VINNIE REAM

BOOKS BY GORDON LANGLEY HALL

Peter Jumping Horse

Peter Jumping Horse at the Stampede

Vinnie Ream:
The Story of the Girl Who Sculptured Lincoln

Vinnie Ream

THE STORY OF THE GIRL

WHO SCULPTURED LINCOLN

BY GORDON LANGLEY HALL

HOLT, RINEHART AND WINSTON

New York · Chicago · San Francisco

For Isabelle Angus
and Brownie Adams

"Who is Vinnie Ream?" *St. Louis News, August, 1866.*

"I am a sculptor, and my life has been a happy one—so happy that I have feared always that I was 'eating my white bread' and that some terrible storm was surely to break over me, for it seemed as if Heaven could not give me so much. My work has never been labor, but an ecstatic delight to my soul. I have worked in my studio not envying kings in their splendor; my mind to me was my kingdom, and my work more than diamonds and rubies."

—From an address given to the International Council of Women, Toronto, Canada, June 30, 1909.

ACKNOWLEDGMENT

I would like to thank the following for their suggestions and kindly help given me during the long period of research necessary for the writing of my book:

Mary Paxton Keeley, author of the play *Little Vinnie Ream*; Maude E. Griffin; Mrs. C. E. Cook, Oklahoma Historical Society; Mrs. Mark P. (Allean) Hale; Eric T. King for tracking down church records in Washington, D.C., Mrs. Joseph Henry (Charlotte) Jackson of Berkeley, California, for encouragement; Patience Ross; Anne Crouch; Joyce Glover, antiquarian bookseller of Eastbourne, England; A. Parks McCombs, M.D., for explaining medical data relating to Vinnie Ream's last illness; Bjørn Ochsner of The Royal Library, Copenhagen, Denmark, who kindly supplied the portrait of George Brandes signed Schemboche Phot—Turin & Florence, taken in Florence, Italy, a few days before his meeting with Vinnie Ream; the Archivist of the United States of America; General Services Administration, National Archives and Records Service, Washington, D.C.; J. D. Haley, Assistant Archivist, the University of Oklahoma; David C. Mearns, Chief, and his staff at the Manuscript Division, the Library of Congress, Washington, D.C.; William J. Petersen, Superintendent, the State Historical Society of Iowa, Iowa City; Lt. Col. Henry Harrison Hall, Ret., Army of the United States of America; J. Metzler, Superintendent, Arlington National Cemetery, Virginia; Kay Wade, Reference Librarian, the State Historical Society of Missouri, Columbia, Missouri; the Charleston Library Society, Charleston, South Carolina; Harold Merklen, Research Librarian, the New York Public Library; William B. Walker, Librarian, The Brooklyn Museum; John D. Morrell, Assistant Librarian,

The Long Island Historical Society, Kings County, New York; William H. Gerdts, Curator of Painting and Sculpture, The Newark Museum, Newark, New Jersey; Gladys L. Krone, Librarian, Carnegie City Library, Fort Smith, Arkansas; Dorothy English, Librarian, Pennsylvania Division, Carnegie Library of Pittsburgh, Pennsylvania; Peggy McCully, Librarian, Christian College, Columbia, Missouri; Georgia Gambrill, Chief, Reference Department, St. Louis Public Library, St. Louis, Missouri; Margaret Gleason, Reference Librarian, The State Historical Society of Wisconsin; Leonard B. Archer, Director, John T. Challoner, Historian, and the staff of Oshkosh Public Library, Oshkosh, Wisconsin; Mrs. Blair Haynes, Reference Librarian, the Public Library of Iowa City, Iowa; Pietro Giancoli, Vital Statistics Section, Government of the District of Columbia, Department of Public Health, Washington, D.C.; Mrs. John Tallman, Receptionist, Washington Cathedral, Washington, D.C.; Dr. Minnie M. Brashear; and my typists Gertrude Young and Gladys Fletcher.

Also to many friends known and unknown who assisted me with courtesy during my searchings in England, France, Denmark, Italy and the U.S.A.

—G.L.H.

CONTENTS

VINNIE REAM

✑ I ✑

THE LEADER OF THE BAND

GUITARS! GUITARS! Who will buy my sweet stringed guitars?"

Robert Lee Ream gingerly edged his way through the crowd of pioneer settlers and Indians to see what all the fuss was about. Behind him, clutching the tail of his coat, was his ten-year-old daughter Vinnie, a smiling wisp of a girl with a mop of chestnut curls. When finally they reached the front, the sight which met their eyes was worth their effort. A red-haired gentleman, sporting a battered top hat and claret-colored vest, was standing at the open flaps of the most unusual covered wagon Vinnie had ever seen. Strung around its sides were strange six-stringed musical instruments. The stranger had obviously driven a long way, thought Vinnie, for his horse looked very weary indeed.

Mr. Ream, a surveyor for the United States government in what was then the remote Wisconsin territory, shouted for the man in the wagon to give them a demonstration. When the man obligingly consented, several Indian women, carrying babies in cradle boards on their backs, started to run. They had never heard guitar music before and, for that matter, neither had Vinnie.

The gentleman having finished his tune, repeated his

call, "Guitars! guitars! Who will buy my sweet stringed guitars?"

The people in the crowd looked inquiringly at one another before Vinnie's father plucked up enough courage to ask how on earth would they be able to play a guitar if they did buy one.

"Simple," explained the stranger, mopping his perspiring face; he would be around for several days to instruct them personally. In addition, to every purchaser he would present a booklet of "easy-to-play" melodies.

Mr. Ream looked at Vinnie. "Would you like one?" he asked.

"Papa, I would rather have the horse," said Vinnie. "It looks so hungry."

The crowd laughed, for everybody knew Vinnie, who on September 24, 1847, had been the first baby girl born in the tiny settlement of what now forms part of Madison, Wisconsin. Like Abraham Lincoln she had first seen the light of day in a log cabin.

Young Vinnie had a weakness for feeding the hungry and caring for the helpless. She was always begging food from her mother to give to the Indian children. She would sit with a papoose on her knee for hours.

Robert Ream smiled, for he could easily picture the startled look upon his thrifty, determined wife's face if he took home another mouth to feed. Lavinia McDonald Ream, of Scottish descent, had been born at Hagerstown, Maryland. Her husband was born at Center County, Pennsylvania, in 1811, and though he was considered to be one of the most accomplished draftsmen in the Surveyor General's Department, he had known both poverty and hardship. At frequent intervals, as his work demanded, he and his family moved from one log cabin to another in the frontier territories.

"I think you had better take the guitar," he advised his daughter. "Think of all the good times we'll have when the evenings are long, listening to you play."

Vinnie nodded her approval, prompted by the fact that she was the only child whose parent was willing to buy one. Five grownups, including an Indian medicine man, also purchased the mysterious instruments. Unfortunately, two nights later the gentleman with the battered top hat disappeared, lock, stock, and hungry horse. Of all his clients, only Vinnie, the youngest, had benefited from his scanty teaching. For hours she would sit in a ring of teepees with an audience of Winnebago children as she diligently strummed on her new guitar.

In three weeks she had mastered all of the airs in the booklet and was ready to expand her musical capabilities. Why, she asked her surprised parents, couldn't she start her own band?

Her father saw no reason why she shouldn't. Her mother said that she never thought she would see the day when Vinnie would take on a full-blooded Indian medicine man as a pupil.

Eventually, all five grownups who had bought the guitars good-naturedly consented to having the precocious ten-year-old as their teacher. Every evening except Sunday they met in her parents' cabin for an hour's instruction in guitar playing. In a surprisingly short time the persevering Vinnie had them all playing in unison, although the medicine man was the only one she could trust with a solo. For the rest of that summer and well into fall, "Little Vin's Musicians" gave many concerts on the Ream cabin porch to an audience arranged informally on the ground in front. As could be expected in a frontier settlement where entertainment was scarce, they were also welcome at parties and hoe-downs.

When Vinnie's naturally proud mother was asked whether her daughter had ever benefited from the tuition of a real music teacher, Mrs. Ream truthfully said, "No." The previous spring Vinnie had visited a tiny convent school in St. Joseph, Missouri, but she had learned nothing more than a few simple songs from the kindly nuns, although they had allowed her to be Queen in a little May Day festival.

The fame of "Little Vin's Musicians" soon traveled to other rural settlements, where in time it reached the ears of a woman who had recently inherited her late sister's piano. Four men were required to lift the piano out of a wagon and carry it into her cabin; but then, not knowing one note from another, she promptly wrote Vinnie a letter:

> Please, Miss Vin, will you kindly come out and play my pi-anna.

That weekend Vinnie's father drove her fifteen miles to the woman's cabin where, from Friday to Sunday, with no other aid than the notes she had learned from her guitar, Vinnie managed to pick out several songs and hymns contained in the books that had come with the piano. The owner was delighted. She actually offered to adopt Vinnie as her own daughter so that the girl could always play to her; but Mrs. Ream, poor as she was, and with two other children to feed—Bob and Cynthia Ann, known to the family as Mary—refused the offer. Instead, she promised that Vinnie might return at intervals to "perform on the splendid instrument."

At this early period of her life Vinnie gave little indication that she would grow up to be a famous sculptress. Her parents and friends believed that her talents lay in the musical field, although it was unthinkable that she should try to earn her living on the stage. For most "respectable families" the world of the theater was still "beyond the pale." In any case, her parents felt that Vinnie, with her effervescent personality, needed discipline. They wanted her to go to school to "learn to be a lady."

Vinnie was sorry to leave the Territory of Wisconsin. She had grown to love its strange rock formations that seemed to have been smoothed and carved by a giant hand. Even then, rocks and stones fascinated her youthful mind, although she did not know why.

In 1857, the appointment of Robert Ream to survey Western Missouri provided the opportunity for Vinnie and Mary to attend Christian College in Columbia. Up to the age of twelve, younger girls could attend the section of the college known as the Academy. Lavinia's thriftiness, augmented with the rent from a paying guest, was just enough to eke out the girls' tuition and boarding fees.

It was an excellent choice of a school, for during her stay, Vinnie was to make friendships that later proved useful. She was a favorite student of the college president, Joseph Kirtley Rogers, who admired her hard work. Studying both instrumental and vocal music, she often took over practice periods for other less enthusiastic girls.

This love of music naturally delighted her teachers. She had brought her guitar to school, in addition to which she was now endeavoring to master the harp, banjo, and harpsichord. Of all these instruments the harp was to become her favorite. Vinnie also proved to be a very good dancer.

Fellow students found her a staunch friend who did not boast of her many achievements. Although she was one of the tiniest girls in the school, she rapidly became a leader. She enjoyed composing her own verses, often turning for inspiration to the Indian lore of earlier days. When Vinnie announced that she was about to write a college song, few doubted that she would succeed. As it turned out, she also composed the music, and President Rogers liked the song so much that for years it was sung by the Academy girls.

As if music and literary talents were not enough, Vinnie also took up painting. She painted a picture of Martha Washington and gave it to the Martha Washington Society, whose recording secretary she was at one time. The picture was hung in the college's administration building.

An important college visitor was Major James Sidney Rollins, later Congressman and an intimate friend of the artist, George Caleb Bingham. Rollins, who was to earn the popular title, "Father of the University of Missouri," had met Vinnie's father during the latter's surveying trips for the government. Delighted at hearing Vinnie described as the best artist in the college and recognizing real talent in her drawings, Rollins advised her to study hard.

Suddenly, Vinnie found herself expressing a wish not to become an artist but a sculptress. Again he encouraged her. The visit of Major Rollins was destined to play an important part in her future life.

When, toward the end of 1858, Vinnie left Christian College, the President gave her a clipping by Robert Hall, English minister and writer (1764-1831), which she was to recall many times during her busy life. It read:

> No man can ever become eminent in anything, unless he work at it with an earnestness bordering on enthusiasm.

❧ 2 ❧

THE CHEROKEE CALLERS

SCHOOL DAYS OVER, Vinnie and Mary rejoined Mr. and Mrs. Ream in their new home at Fort Smith, Arkansas. Situated on the Arkansas River at the Oklahoma line, this fast-growing town had been founded as a military post in 1817. During the gold rush days of 1848, it had become an important outfitting point for those on their way to California in seach of a quick fortune.

Vinnie liked the hustle and bustle of Fort Smith, where she soon found herself singing at church socials. Her father, worn out by hardships from his years of mapping new lands in frontier territories, had formed with Judge John Carnall the real-estate firm of Carnall and Ream. Vinnie's artistic abilities were put to good use when she helped to color maps in her father's office. Judge Carnall suggested that she should be sent to study art in Italy, but such an expenditure was out of the question.

Across the Arkansas River lay Indian territory inhabited by the five Indian "nations"—Cherokee, Choctaw, Chickasaw, Creek, and Seminole—who, during the 1820's, had been forced to leave their ancestral homes in the southeastern states for new lands in what is now part of Oklahoma. The Cherokees had formerly occupied the upper valley of the Tennessee River.

Vinnie, who had grown up among them, had always liked Indians. In an age not noted for its humanity toward these first Americans, she was always their sympathetic friend. Thirteen years old, rosy cheeked, and with eyes so brown that men often called them black, she was already an extremely attractive young woman. As Lavinia, her mother, sometimes said, "Our Vinnie is growing up."

Vinnie, both coquettish and intelligent, soon learned that she was attractive to the opposite sex. As she grew older, it was remarked, sometimes unkindly, that she could twist a man around her little finger.

Two important names emerge from her Fort Smith days: Elias Cornelius Boudinot (1835-1890) and John Rollin Ridge (1827-1867). They were both Cherokee Indians who, while visiting Vinnie's father, had been captivated by his younger daughter.

Elias Boudinot (Vinnie nicknamed him Boudy) was a lawyer, born in the Cherokee nation at New Echota, Georgia. His father, another Elias, had been assassinated in 1839. Elias was sent to live with one of his mother's, Harriet Gold's, sisters at Manchester, Vermont. After working as an engineer on a railroad in Ohio, Boudy had settled in Fayetteville, Arkansas, where he studied law and was called to the bar in 1856. In addition to his practice, he did editorial work for the *Arkansian*. He became chairman of the Democratic state central committee, and was soon appointed chief editorial writer for Little Rock's *True Democrat*.

Boudy was twenty-five when he first came calling at

the Ream's residence. The difference in his age and Vinnie's did not seem to mar their friendship—on her part rather a whimsical one—though there seems little doubt that the dashing Boudy fell in love with her. Her quick wit and sharp brain intrigued him as much as her charming appearance. Although their political discussions, conducted on the front porch, often ended in heated arguments, Boudy always came back.

Boudy's rival for Vinnie's affections was his cousin, a talented young Cherokee named John Rollin Ridge, son of Chief John Ridge. He was eight years older than Boudy, but his gentle ways endeared him to the vivacious Vinnie. A poet and journalist, his collected poems were later published.

His friendship for Vinnie prompted her to write several poems herself. Deposited among her family papers in the Library of Congress, there are several poems with Indian themes, including a nostalgic piece called "Spirit Lake."

Robert Ream's business enterprise in Fort Smith was not so successful as he had hoped it would be. Deciding, because of his past employment with the government, that his best hopes for the future lay in Washington, D.C., he decided to move his family there. John Ridge was heartbroken when he learned that Vinnie would be going away. She, too, was sorry, having become very attached to the kind and talented man.

"You have written some beautiful poems," she told

him. "I want you to write one for me as a parting gift which I shall keep always."

John Ridge fulfilled her request. Next morning he handed her the verses of "I Love Thee," which later she set to music.

I love thee, as the soaring bird
    The bright blue morning, when he sings,
In circling melodies,
    With Heaven's sweet sunlight on his wings.

I love thee, as the mariner,
    Far driven o'er a stormy sea,
The silver rising star
    Which tells him where his home may be.

I love thee as the billows love
    In tropic lands the pearly shore;
They come and go
    With answering kisses evermore!

I love thee. Ever, ever shall
    Thine eyes' dark, glorious light
Dwell in my soul,
    Illumining its deeps of night.

3

VINNIE GOES TO WASHINGTON

THE REAM FAMILY reached Washington, D.C., during the
first year of the War Between the States. On April 12, 1861,
the Confederates had fired on Fort Sumter, South Carolina.

It was not the best time for a family to settle in Washington, but Robert Ream saw no alternative. Far from
well, he was nevertheless assured of work as a part-time
map-maker with the army because of his good record in
government service.

To Vinnie, the nation's capital seemed a madhouse
after the quiet of Columbia and Fort Smith. The family
got off the train at the dilapidated railroad depot where
hundreds of troops detrained daily to encamp in and
around the city, bringing dirt and litter in their wake.
Vinnie gazed wide-eyed at the gun carriages, army wagons,
and quartermasters' trains that crowded the dusty streets.
As she drove with her parents down Pennsylvania Avenue,
with its meager covering of thin cobblestones, their hired
carriage was guided gingerly along to avoid the ruts and
potholes. The cries of wounded and dying soldiers came
from makeshift hospitals that had sprung up like mush-
rooms overnight. Above the din Vinnie could hear fish
and oyster venders loudly shouting their wares.

Squealing pigs, angry geese, chickens, and ducks added

to the general confusion as they roamed the streets searching for garbage. Vinnie thought the carriage would never reach their rooming house. Then, suddenly, the driver called their attention to the solitary man who, with stovepipe hat and old shawl about his shoulders, determinedly picked his way through the crowded street. It was *Abraham Lincoln.* Vinnie Ream would never forget this, her first glimpse of the man who was President of the United States. As he strode freely among the crowds to the consternation of his guards, who feared for his safety, she was struck "by the lines of sadness on his face."

Later, when the family was safely installed in temporary quarters for the night, Mr. Ream answered Vinnie's eager questions about the city. He told her that, between the years 1800-1860, it had grown into a city of some sixty-six thousand inhabitants. Of the nation's capital at this period, Anthony Trollope, the English novelist and son of the critical Mrs. Trollope, who had written a book entitled *The Domestic Manners of the Americans,* commented disparagingly:

> Tucking up your trousers you will wade through the bogs, you will lose yourself among rude hillocks, you will be out of the reach of humanity.

Vinnie soon learned that Washington was more like a Southern city than a Northern one, Confederate sentiment being strong there. Many sons from Washington's finest families had actually gone South to enlist in the army. Although her parents were staunch in the Union cause, soon after their arrival Vinnie's brother Bob had quietly slipped off one night to join a rebel cavalry regiment.

To complicate matters, her beloved Boudy wrote that he, too, was joining the Confederate forces. Vinnie sat right down to pen him a letter of protestation, for in the matter of loyalty she had sided with her parents. She was learning early in the strife that civil war could be a terrible affair, splitting families and turning brother against brother. When people spoke unkindly of "that impossible woman"—the President's wife—Vinnie's heart ached with sympathy for Mary Todd Lincoln. Surely, thought Vinnie, with so many relatives fighting for the Southern cause, she suffered torments similar to her own. Should Vinnie be loyal to Bob and Boudy or to her parents?

Yet there was no time to brood, for other, more pressing, personal matters were at hand. Her thrifty mother found Washington an expensive place in which to live. Mr. Ream's salary was still inadequate, so Mary, Vinnie's elder sister, was forced to take a position in the land office.

To help them financially, Senator Edmund G. Ross of Kansas, an old acquaintance of Robert Ream, came to board with them. Ross was a pleasant addition to their household. He was always ready to answer Vinnie's countless questions concerning Washington's social life. They soon became great friends, for she was never ill at ease with older people.

Unfortunately, even with the extra income derived from the Senator's rent, Lavinia was hard put to make ends meet. It was then that Vinnie, not quite fifteen years old and weighing only ninety pounds, begged permission from her parents to look for work. With some misgivings they consented, and she obtained a clerk's job in the post office, replacing a man who had gone off to war. Her salary was fifty dollars a month.

Looking rather like marble palaces, the Post Office building and the Patent Office (which boasted an intriguing exhibition of models and curiosities) stood diagonally across from each other at Seventh and F streets. Henry Adams once compared them to ". . . Greek temples in the abandoned gravelpits of a deserted Syrian city."

Vinnie was popular among her fellow workers. She listened avidly as they gossiped about such famous personages as Mr. and Mrs. Tom Thumb, the famous dwarfs who, married at Grace Church in New York's Greenwich Village, had recently been visiting Washington's well-known Willard's Hotel. They spoke of Clara Barton, the "Florence Nightingale" of America, and Mrs. Rose O'Neal Greenhow, the Washington hostess who had become a celebrated Confederate spy. At the end of August, her house, where she had been kept under close arrest, was turned into a women's prison, jokingly called "Fort Greenhow" by the tourists. Vinnie was determined to pass it during one of her walks through the city.

Although Washington was described as "a city of magnificent distances," she found sightseeing easier than might have been expected, because it was possible to visit the Capitol, Executive Mansion, Treasury, Post Office, Patent Office, and the Smithsonian Institution with its tasteful gardens all in a morning.

Of these, Vinnie found the classic Capitol, with its half-finished dome, the most interesting. Fearful of the outcome of the war, other people were not so enthusiastic, for with persistent rumors that Washington would be attacked by the rebels, the uncompleted dome seemed to many like a premonition of doom. The fine collection of paintings and statuary inside the building delighted Vinnie's artistic eye. Fellow visitors were amused to see the pretty girl, wearing a small hat topped with two enormous white roses, reverently touching the cool smoothness of the sculptured marble.

Many of her fellow Americans might find the Senate Chamber decorations, together with the red and gold of the Hall of Representatives, overly ornate, foreign, and gaudy, but not Vinnie. She loved them, already dreaming of the days when the war would be over and the gleaming wings of the Capitol completed. Only the sight of great blocks of marble, key capitals, and partially finished carvings scattered over the ground among workmen's sheds was depressing to her young eyes.

Out on the Capitol's East Portico she once gazed for an hour at Persico's Columbus and the other enormous statues. The statue of George Washington by Horatio Greenough (1805-1852), the Boston sculptor, claimed her special attention, though she was forced to admit that the

Father of his Country looked strangely unnatural, naked to the waist, his limbs dripping with draperies! Greenough might have modeled him upon the Roman idea of Jupiter Tonans, but outspoken Vinnie told her parents that night over supper that if she had been the sculptor, Washington would have been garbed in his regular clothing instead of some borrowed from Italy!

She was not alone in her criticism, for even Philip's popular guidebook of the period conceded that the first President was "scarcely recognizable in this garb, to his countrymen." Sitting there among the other giant monuments, he looked even more outlandish.

There was also the Library of Congress and its marble extension to be explored, and, of course, the Executive Mansion where Madame President was as negligent for her own safety as her husband was for his. Vinnie soon found that it was possible to inspect the first-floor parlors without interference, for no watchman was on duty. Because of this, costly furnishings were often stolen or simply carried off as souvenirs. Sweethearts and vandals carved hearts and initials on priceless woodwork and tables.

Mrs. Lincoln saw no reason, even in wartime, to have the front door closed until late at night. Sometimes of an evening the more enterprising "uninvited visitors" even found their way upstairs to see the family quarters.

The Executive Mansion resembled a Southern plantation home more than anything else. There were greenhouses and kitchen gardens in the rear, while an iron fence with impressive gateways enclosed the front. On the south, the grounds were protected by yet another fence. The lawns were crisscrossed by linking paths, with the one to the north open to public use. Andrew J. Downing, the horticulturist, along with others from the Smithsonian Institution, had been responsible for planning the White House gardens.

Snipe, Vinnie was told, could still be shot in full view of the White House, which was unfortunately located close to the Potomac flats, said to be the reason for the persistence of malaria in the city during the hot months of summer and fall. The marsh at the foot of the President's Park was once used as a sewage outlet. Close by, lay the opening of the old city canal, formerly called the Tiber. Since falling into disuse, it had become a convenient dumping place for dead animals, sewage, and every conceivable form of garbage. To reach the important, if unfinished, Mall, a visitor had to cross this offensive-smelling waterway by one of several high iron bridges.

Among high weeds, directly south of the President's home, stood one third of the shaft that was being erected in memory of George Washington. Many patriotic Americans, like Vinnie, picked their way through the high grass and loose, unplaced stonework, muttering at the ingratitude of those who had not persevered in continuing the subscription drive for its completion.

North of Pennsylvania Avenue was a prosperous and fashionable section of the city. The area to the south was dingy and poor. The Center Market was south of the avenue, with its motley conglomeration of sheds backed on the same unhealthy common sewer, the old canal.

As was to be expected, the prosperous north side boasted the best restaurants, stores, and hotels, including the famed Willard's, a popular meeting place for important families. There the ladies, at that time not in the least calory-conscious, sat down to gargantuan meals, often out-eating their husbands!

A young English clerk at the British Embassy wrote disapprovingly to his mother of the American women who enjoyed breakfasts of "fried oysters, steak, and onions, blancmange and pâté de foie gras," followed by a large midday dinner, an equally substantial one at five, tea at seven-thirty, and another supper "to last them for the night" at nine. Vinnie, like the other young women working at the Post Office, avidly listened to such stories of life in "high society." She was determined to visit Willard's herself one day—if she could find somebody generous enough to take her.

Senator Ross told Vinnie that Pennsylvania Avenue had been designed so that the grandeur of the Capitol should be directly visible from the Executive Mansion, but that force of circumstances had changed the plan. The huge Treasury building, he said, had been the cause for a bend in "the" Avenue. As a result, the Capitol overlooked President Buchanan's red-bricked barn on the White House grounds.

One day, while exploring the Rotunda of the Capitol, Vinnie came unexpectedly upon Congressman James S.

Rollins, who at Christian College had been so favorably impressed with her drawings and to whom she had confided that one day she would like to be a sculptress.

Congressman Rollins, always interested in higher education for the women as well as the men of Missouri, had promised the College president that if he should meet his former student, Vinnie Ream, in Washington he would get her picture for him. Vinnie was flattered and readily consented. While they were talking, Vinnie impressed Rollins by her knowledge of the sculpture in Washington. She seemed to remember details that the ordinary visitor would forget. Thinking to improve her knowledge even further, he asked if she would like to accompany him to the studio of his friend Clark Mills (1810-1883), then the foremost sculptor in America.

Vinnie could hardly believe her ears, for nothing in Washington had pleased her so much as Mills's equestrian statue of Andrew Jackson, which stood in Lafayette Square. She was particularly intrigued by the unique engineering feat by which the artist was able to portray Jackson's horse rearing upon its hind legs. Congress had commissioned Mills to make the statue for the sum of twelve thousand dollars, later voting him an extra twenty thousand dollars. They even appropriated the cannon captured by General Jackson at the Battle of New Orleans for the bronze casting, an art then almost unknown in the United States.

Mills had had a romantic and colorful career. As an orphan boy of thirteen, he had run away from his uncle's home in Onondaga County, New York, because of ill-treatment. Eventually reaching South Carolina, he studied to be an ornamental plasterer. John C. Calhoun, twice Vice-President of the United States, was among the outstanding Southerners who commissioned him to make clay (or plaster) busts of themselves.

Delighted with the results, Calhoun and several influential friends subscribed the money to send young Mills to study abroad. Vinnie had known that the nationally famous sculptor had a studio and foundry in Washington, but there seemed almost no chance of her ever visiting them. Now, Congressman Rollins had provided the key. Impulsively taking his arm, she walked proudly with him in the direction of the studio.

A STEP TO THE WHITE HOUSE

CLARK MILLS was preparing some clay when his visitors arrived. A man of middle age, he had a winning way with the ladies, Vinnie proving to be no exception. She was charmed with his manners for, in spite of his fame, he was not proud. When told by the enthusiastic Rollins that his pretty young friend had ambitions to be a sculptress, Mills did not laugh. Instead, he tossed Vinnie a lump of clay which she narrowly missed catching.

"Do a portrait of me!" he suggested, and to his surprise she sat down at a bench and immediately went to work.

The result was crude, but such a good try that Mills suggested she choose a more familiar subject. Vinnie's quick mind thought first of her Cherokee friends Boudy and John Ridge as possible subjects. Handsome Boudy would look fine modeled in clay, she thought, until she remembered that she had "temporarily fallen out with him" because of his Confederate allegiance.

Then she recalled her childhood days out on the frontier. "A Wisconsin Indian . . . the very thing." Helping herself liberally to the clay that Mills had prepared for his next subject, Vinnie began deftly to fashion her subject. Fascinated by such natural talent, Mills watched carefully as a fine Indian head complete with feathers rapidly took shape. When Vinnie left the studio, her best Scottish gingham dress somewhat soiled from her efforts, she had an invitation to return whenever she liked as a student-helper. Vinnie, again not on the merits of beauty alone, had made another conquest.

Vinnie's parents were rather apprehensive of Mills's offer, for were not sculptresses regarded in the same unfavorable light as actresses? A properly brought up girl of that mid-Victorian era looked forward only to the possibility of a suitable marriage. Any woman who wanted a career was immediately suspected of favoring the fight for women's rights. Even in proper Boston the "dreadful" reformer, Lucy Stone, was leading a fight for women's rights in what was then very definitely a man's world. Although in 1855 Lucy did condescend to marry a member of the opposition, Henry B. Blackwell, she reserved the right to keep her maiden name.

"Are you intending to be another Lucy Stone?" Lavinia Ream now asked her budding sculptress a little tearfully.

Mr. Ream only shrugged his shoulders, knowing that in the end Vinnie would get her own way, for she could charm the pearl out of an oyster. He reminded his wife that there were some very fine sculptresses such as Harriet Hosmer from Massachusetts and Emma Stebbins of New York City. Both had brought honor to their country and their sex. Harriet, a very religious woman, had struggled to obtain the education in anatomy necessary for her vocation. Emma, a native of New York City, first learned oil painting from Henry Inman, later taking up work in clay and marble. Her exquisite fountain in the form of an angel stood in New York's Central Park. Surely, countered Vinnie's father, these women had not disgraced their names by sculpturing.

"But they studied in Rome. . . . We are poor." Mrs. Ream, who had spent all day making over old drapes to hang at the windows of their new home on Capitol Hill, knew what she was talking about. It was a sore point with her that her daughters had been forced to take employment at all.

In the end, a compromise was reached. Vinnie could study with Clark Mills, but not until she was sixteen. Somewhat amused, Clark, whose latest work was the casting of Thomas Crawford's colossal statue, "Armed Freedom," which was to stand on top of the Capitol's unfinished dome, assured her that he was willing to wait.

He was more patient than his prospective pupil, whose restless spirit inveigled some Catholic sisters into giving her lessons on the harp.

"She is so like an angel," they said, "that we couldn't refuse her."

The nuns were shocked one day to find their "angel" playing a piece suggestively called "I Love Thee." Her large brown eyes filled with innocence, she seriously told them that it had been dedicated to her by a Cherokee Indian!

Vinnie broke another barrier into territory formerly

reserved only for men and boys by becoming the first
woman choir singer in a local church. Her scrapbooks re-
veal that she received the sum of three hundred dollars a
year for her singing.

Vinnie was sixteen in the September of 1863, and, true
to their promise, her parents allowed her to study in Clark
Mills's studio. She did not give up her position at the Post
Office at once, but continued to work there part-time. Her
legible handwriting, diligently practiced at Christian
College, enabled her to take part in Washington's enormous Sanitary Fair, held to benefit the Sanitary Commission which raised funds to provide comforts for the Union
troops.

Printed handbills proclaimed:

VINNIE REAM

IN CHARGE OF THE

POST OFFICE

GRAND SANITARY FAIR

Contributions of Stationery and Unsealed Letters
gratefully received by her
at No. 325 North B Street,
between Delaware Avenue and 1st Street,
Capitol Hill, Washington, D.C.

Vinnie's Post Office booth was an unprecedented success. She collected so much stationery for the boys in
blue that it took several horse-drawn vans to cart it away!

On Saturday evening, October 17th, Vinnie, together
with others who had helped at the Fair, were invited to attend Grover's Theater where Charlotte Saunders Cushman, a well-known actress, was giving her much-celebrated

performance as Lady Macbeth. James William Wallack, Jr., played Macbeth, assisted by Edward Loomis Davenport as Macduff. President and Mrs. Lincoln watched from their special box. For years, Vinnie treasured her copy of the program, fringed in lace, bordered in blue, and printed upon white satin.

Lincoln, who was delighted with his evening's entertainment, had written a few months previously, "I think nothing equals Macbeth."

The *Evening Star* of Washington, on Monday, October 19, 1863, faithfully described the dazzling event:

> The benefit in aid of the Sanitary Commission, at Grover's Saturday night was a great success, netting over $2,000 for the object proposed. President Lincoln, Mrs. Lincoln, Master Thady (Thomas) Lincoln, and Mr. (William O.) Stoddard, the President's Secretary, occupied the lower stage boxes to the right, and Secretary Seward, Lord Lyons (British Minister) and others of note, those opposite. Every part of the house was jammed, and reserved seats sold at a large premium long before the hour of opening.

Wide-eyed, Vinnie watched approvingly as Miss Cushman was called before the curtain at the close of the play to be "honored" according to the *Daily National Republican* in Washington, "with an elegant bouquet from the ladies in Mr. Seward's box."

In addition to her work at the Post Office, Vinnie found time to become a part-time voluntary visitor to military hospitals. There she did some practical nursing, sang to the wounded, played her guitar, wrote letters for those men too sick to write home, and comforted the dying. Visiting the inadequate, makeshift hospitals was a grim job. Often, she returned home nauseated by the smell of sickness and death. Girls on both sides of the conflict were doing equally valiant work among their own wounded.

On one of her hospital visits Vinnie met General Ulysses S. Grant, who commended her singing, as did several other prominent Northern generals.

It infuriated Vinnie to think as she walked home exhausted from her volunteer nursing that with Washington actually threatened by attack, still black marketeers abounded; army contracts could be bought by the unscrupulous; and fortunes were being made by the manufacturers of poor-quality blankets and uniforms, leaky boots, and bad food.

During the war years, Vinnie took part in several important musical performances, including the *Grand Concert* held in Lincoln General Hospital on May 3, 1864. She was listed as one of "the following amateurs (who) have volunteered their services for the occasion." In honor of her mother's Scottish ancestry, she sang "Annie Laurie" as a solo. With a friend, Emma Bartlet, she rendered an appropriate duet, "I Cannot Bid Thee Go, My Boy." Afterward, Emma inquired why Vinnie had gone off key right in the middle, but did not receive a satisfactory answer. The truth was that Vinnie had been singing to her fellow Yankees, but thinking of Boudy, her Confederate friend. Returning to Indian territory, he had been elected delegate to the Confederate Congress for the Territory, and the following year he had helped Stand Waitie raise an Indian regiment.

Boudy! Would he never cease to haunt her dreams? In spite of their falling out, she often remembered him wistfully.

A HEAD OF MR. LINCOLN

THE WAR between the States was over; the men would be coming home. On March 4, 1865, Abraham Lincoln had been inaugurated to his second term as President. General Robert E. Lee had surrendered on April 9th to General Ulysses S. Grant at Appomattox Courthouse, Virginia.

Vinnie's studies with Clark Mills had proved very successful. Mills, a good teacher, was proud of his young pupil's steady progress. After a while, knowing that she needed money to enable her to study full-time, he arranged that she might accept portrait commissions. He was encouraging when she spoke of her "dearest ambition" to make a head of no less a personage than Mr. Lincoln himself. From the first day when Vinnie had seen the President in stovepipe hat and shawl walking unguarded among the people, she had been fascinated by this "man of sorrows." Now, when she watched him drive through the streets of Washington in his carriage, attended on either side by uniformed cavalrymen, the desire to perpetuate his features in clay became almost an obsession. Often, after catching such a fleeting glimpse of him, she would rush back to the studio and vainly attempt to mold his likeness. At last, in desperation, she approached her old friend Congressman Rollins of Missouri. Did he think that President Lincoln might sit for her while working at his desk in the White House? She would be "as quiet as a mouse."

Instead of laughing at her presumption, Rollins was delighted with Vinnie's fulfillment as a sculptor and, in conjunction with Senator Orville H. Browning of Illinois, appealed personally to the President to grant the young girl's request.

At that time, Vinnie knew, both Abraham and Mary Todd Lincoln were still recovering from a great family sorrow, the loss of their eleven-year-old son Willie (William Wallace Lincoln), who had died February 20, 1862, from typhoid fever. Lincoln, for the most part, was able to control his outward expressions of sorrow, but not his wife. Her grief for the blue-eyed youngster could only find an outlet in sudden outbursts of hysteria and weeping. Elizabeth Keckley, the Negro mantua maker who was the First Lady's favorite dressmaker, said that Mrs. Lincoln was unable to look at Willie's picture or ever enter again the bedroom where he died. Mrs. Keckley had once seen Mr. Lincoln lead his prostrate wife to the window, where, pointing toward the grim battlements of a sanitarium, he said in a kindly voice, "Mother, do you see that large white building on the hill yonder? Try and control your grief, or it will drive you mad, and we may have to send you there."

Lincoln, himself a man of humble beginnings, was intrigued by the story of the poor Post Office clerk who had been accepted as a pupil by so eminent a sculptor as Clark Mills. The President had no daughters of his own, a fact he obviously regretted, for on October 19, 1860, in reply to a letter sent to him by little Grace Bedell, aged eleven, of Westfield, New York, he said: "I regret the necessity of saying I have no daughters."

Toward the end of 1864, Vinnie sent her tools and a large tub of clay to the White House, then put on her best dress (but she made sure to take a large checked apron to protect it) and hurried off to keep her first appointment with the President of the United States. She graphically described in her diary the half-hourly visits she paid to the White House during the next five months:

> I was a mere slip of a child, weighing less than ninety pounds and the contrast between the rawboned man and me was indeed great. I sat in my corner and begged Mr. Lincoln not to allow me to disturb him. He seemed to find a sort of companionship in being with me, although we talked but little. His favorite son, Willie, had just died and this had been the greatest personal loss in his life. I made him think of Willie and he often said so and as often wept. I remember him especially in two attitudes. The first was with his great form slouched down into a chair at his desk, his head bowed upon his chest, deeply thoughtful. I think he was with his generals on the battlefields, appraising the horrible sacrifices brought upon his people and the nation. The second was at the window watching for Willie, for he had always watched the boy playing every afternoon at that window. Sometimes great tears rolled down his cheeks . . .

I think that history is particularly correct in writing about Abraham Lincoln to describe him as a man of unfathomable sorrow. That was the lasting impression I always had of him. It was this I put into my statue, for when he sat for me he let himself go and fell into the mood that was ever with him, but against which he struggled. He never told a funny story and he rarely smiled.

He had been painted and modeled before, but when he learned that I was poor, he granted me the sittings for no other purpose than that I was a poor girl. Had I been the greatest sculptor in the world, I am sure that he would have refused at that time.

Mrs. Lincoln once told General Adam Badeau, "Do you know, sir, that I never permit the President to see any woman alone?" Yet apparently she had no objection to her husband's sitting for Vinnie Ream, although the girl was only seventeen years old and in the full bloom of youth.

Mary Todd Lincoln, then in her forties and ten years younger than her husband, was not easy to satisfy where her own likeness was concerned. Vinnie was thankful that she was not making a head of the woman, who had once ordered the photographer, Matthew B. Brady, to destroy all the negatives he ever made of her. She was still pleasantly plump, "Like a wind-blown rose." Vinnie thought her neck particularly attractive.

Criticized by her enemies on account of what they termed her "wild extravagances, gaucherie and insane jealousy," Mrs. Lincoln was naturally possessive of her husband. Perhaps she felt a mutual bond with the girl sculptress, for they had several things in common. Both were keenly interested in visiting hospitals to lessen the sufferings of wounded soldiers. Like Vinnie, Mrs. Lincoln had a tender heart. When, in 1861, she had heard that a young soldier, William Scott, was to be shot for falling asleep on picket duty she "grew so nervous" that the President actually told General McClellan that "the Lady President" greatly hoped the man would be pardoned. He was!

With Vinnie, she shared the worry of having loved ones serving in the opposing Southern armies. However, unlike Vinnie, she had the added strain of being married to the President of the United States. There were many who even questioned her patriotism and loyalty. One brother, George Rogers Clark Todd, was a surgeon with the Confederate army. Her half-brother, Samuel Briggs Todd, a Confederate soldier, was killed at the battle of Shiloh; another half-brother, David H. Todd, died from wounds received at Vicksburg, and yet another, her beloved red-headed Alexander H. Todd, lost his life at Baton Rouge, Louisiana.

Vinnie's brother was still serving in the Confederate cavalry, while her friend Boudy, a Confederate lieutenant colonel, was about to take part in the restoration of peaceful relations between the Cherokees and the United States.

Tad (Thomas) Lincoln, then a boy of nearly twelve, often visited his father's study while Vinnie was at work to see how the "head" was progressing. He was generally accompanied on these occasions by his possessive and overly solicitous mother. Vinnie noted his long, grownup gold watch-chain and neatly parted hair.

On the afternoon of Good Friday, April 14, 1865,

Vinnie worked as usual for half an hour at the White House. The clay model was nearly finished. More than once, Lincoln graciously told her how pleased he was by her efforts. Vinnie little realized that she would be the last sculptor to perpetuate the likeness—etched deeply with lines of grief, compassion, and sympathy—of the Great Emancipator.

That evening, he was going to Ford's Theater with Mrs. Lincoln and their oldest son, Robert Todd Lincoln, who was home from the Union Army. They were to see a new comedy *Our American Cousin*, starring Laura Keene, which had been written by Tom Taylor. Vinnie bade Mr. Lincoln good-bye, hoping that Mrs. Lincoln and he would enjoy the performance. She never saw him alive again.

A strange calm seemed to have fallen over the city. Vinnie was alone in the house, quietly pasting pictures into her new blue-bound scrapbook. After supper her parents had taken a walk together. Upon returning, they were about to open their front door when a man ran past shouting:

"LINCOLN HAS BEEN SHOT! LINCOLN HAS BEEN SHOT!"

Suddenly, to Vinnie, it seemed that all was chaos and commotion. Soldiers on horseback clattered noisily over the cobblestones of Pennsylvania Avenue; guards were posted outside the homes of all important government officials. A seething, threatening mob gathered in front of

Ford's Theater, screaming, "Burn the theater, burn the theater."

During the performance, a little after 10:00 P.M., the President had been shot in the back of the head by John Wilkes Booth, who had then managed to escape. Lincoln was carried across the street to William Peterson's boarding house at 453 Tenth Street. At twenty-one minutes, fifty-five seconds past seven the next morning, Abraham Lincoln, sixteenth President of the United States, was dead.

Vinnie was prostrate with grief. It did not seem possible that only a few hours before she had been in his company at the White House. For several days she suffered from a severe case of shock. From friends, she later heard the tragic details of all that had occurred since the actual assassination.

On that awful night, rumor was rife in Washington that the Vice-President had also been killed, General Grant murdered on a train, the entire Cabinet wiped out.

Next morning, rain fell on Mary Lincoln's head as she was led to a waiting carriage. Upon seeing the theater, scene of the tragedy, she screamed hysterically, "Oh, that dreadful house! That dreadful house!"

Now thought Vinnie, there would be no patient husband to calm her fears and forebodings.

Lincoln's body had been placed in a long coffin and taken to the White House. Behind it a group of army officers walked with their heads bare. Women and children sobbed as the solemn procession passed; hundreds of Negroes, their clothing sodden with rain, stood weeping in front of the Executive Mansion. This was the Great Emancipator's homecoming. The search was on for the fugitive Booth. Mounted policemen and grim-faced cavalrymen had galloped off in search of him in neighboring Maryland. On April 26th, the fugitive, who had broken a leg fleeing from the theater, was shot to death in a burning tobacco barn near Bowling Green, Virginia.

Easter Sunday had dawned bright and sunny in contrast to the night of black Good Friday. As Vinnie lay on a couch in the living room, she heard the singing of birds. Spring had really arrived; the air was sweet with the scent of flowers, yet she felt no joy. The city was hung with endless festoons of black crêpe; Lincoln's picture was in every shop window. Andrew Johnson, the former tailor, was now President of the United States.

On Tuesday, Vinnie, accompanied by her parents, had been among the hundreds of mourners who had filed past the catafalque in the East Room of the Executive Mansion where Lincoln lay in state. The mirrors were veiled; the rich crimson damask drapes camouflaged with black. The central chandelier had been removed, owing to the height of the bier; the remaining two chandeliers hung entwined with lengths of crêpe like huge grotesque birds' nests. Vinnie noted in her writings that Lincoln's casket was "studded with silver nails that glittered like stars where the sunlight touched them."

Friday came and Vinnie was among the silent crowds that watched the casket being placed on the train for the long, roundabout journey to Springfield, Illinois. She wept at the sight of a much-smaller casket, containing Willie's body, which had been placed at Lincoln's feet. It had been taken from the cemetery vault where it had rested since Willie's death. No more, she thought, would the President stand by the window and weep for Willie, as she had seen him do so many times in life. Now they were together forever.

❦6❧

THE DRAGON OF THE HESPERIDES

LINCOLN WAS hardly in his grave before all Washington was talking of the life-size statue of the late President to be placed in the Rotunda of the Capitol. Every established sculptor in the country was eager to receive the exciting commission.

Vinnie first heard the news from Senator Ross, who was still the family boarder. He suggested that she put in an application for the coveted task. After all, he asked her, had she not been the last person to model President Lincoln from life?

"But I'm a woman," was Vinnie's immediate reaction, for Congress had never awarded such an artistic plum to a member of the female sex.

Lavinia Ream, now proud of her daughter's growing talent, prodded Vinnie to accept the Senator's challenge. The girl quickly decided that she would try. With Ross's help she composed her letter of application to Congress, describing in simple language how Lincoln had befriended her.

However, she was not the only woman to make such an application. Harriet Hosmer, the Massachusetts sculptress, did so, too, with the backing of the most powerful woman newspaper columnist of her generation, Mrs. Jane Grey Swisshelm.

After inheriting a legacy from her mother, Mrs. Swisshelm started a publication called *The Pittsburgh Saturday Visitor*. Later, in the course of Andrew Johnson's administration, when she was working as a clerk in a government office, she started a radical paper called the *Reconstructionist*. In this, she attacked the President so vehemently that in 1866 he dismissed her from government service.

"Beware of Sister Jane," was the slogan of contemporary editors. Her most notable attack was made in 1850 through her personal column which appeared in many newspapers. It was on Daniel Webster's private life, and she always believed that it ruined his chances of becoming president.

Mrs. Swisshelm was divorced for desertion by her long-suffering husband, and her life is described by the nineteenth-century biographer, Phebe A. Hannaford, in her book *Daughters of America*, as being one of "shadow and struggle and triumph." Mrs. Swisshelm herself once declared, "Oh! But it is good to have lived and suffered and worked . . . nothing can go wrong with us if only we are right."

When she espoused the cause of Harriet Hosmer and some lesser-known sculptors, there were many who believed that if a woman should be chosen—and it was a big IF—then it was certain to be Harriet. Nobody in the press seems to have even considered Vinnie Ream a possibility

—or even to have heard of her. Little wonder that when, out of the blue, an unknown girl was awarded the honor of the Lincoln statue contract in preference to such established sculptors as her former teacher, Clark Mills, to say nothing of Mrs. Swisshelm's Harriet, the nation's press demanded to know, "WHO IS VINNIE REAM?"

When, on January 28, 1866, Vinnie was actually instructed by Congress to make the coveted piece, she became the first woman ever to receive a contract from the people of the United States to make a statue. Who actually spoke on Vinnie's behalf in government circles is not known, but Senator Ross was much respected and it may have been he. He would have had many influential friends who could have been persuaded to put in a favorable word for his protégée.

The contract, signed by both James Harlan, Secretary of the Interior, and Vinnie Ream, read as follows:

> This agreement made and entered into this 30th day of August, 1866, between James Harlan, Secretary of the Interior, by and on behalf of the United States, pursuant to the authority and direction of a joint resolution entitled "Joint Resolution authorizing a contract with Vinnie Ream for a statue of Abraham Lincoln," approved, July 28th, 1866, of the first part, Vinnie Ream of the City of Washington and District of Columbia, of the second part, witnesseth:
>
> That the said Vinnie Ream for and in consideration of the sum of ten thousand dollars, to be paid to her as hereinafter mentioned, hereby binds herself to execute and deliver to the Commissioner of Public

Buildings, or other public officer, to be designated by the Secretary of the Interior, and in said city, a life-size model and a statue of the late President Lincoln; said statue to be in marble and to the acceptance of such Secretary; and the said Harlan, Secretary as aforesaid in the name and on behalf of said United States, hereby promises to pay to said Vinnie Ream, the sum of Five Thousand Dollars, on the completion as aforesaid of such model in Plaster; and the further sum of Five Thousand Dollars, on the completion to the acceptance of the then Secretary of the Interior, of such life-size statue in marble, and delivery of the same as hereinbefore mentioned.

Witness the hands of the said James Harlan, Secretary of the Interior, and of the said Vinnie Ream, on the day and year aforesaid.

Ten thousand dollars in those days was a small fortune. While Vinnie was exuberant with joy, her parents were flabbergasted to think that such an honor had come to their younger daughter. Moving to Washington, they decided, had not been such a catastrophe after all.

Unfortunately, Vinnie's good fortune made enemies besides friends for her. Nobody was more hostile or vitriolic toward her than Mrs. Swisshelm.

Mrs. Swisshelm obviously considered her opinions of Vinnie Ream to be *right*, although by her own admission she saw her but once ". . . in the Senate gallery putting her ten thousand dollar bill through that body." Yet, writing in the Liberty *Tribune* (Missouri), September 14, 1866, Mrs. Swisshelm declared:

Miss Minnie [sic] Ream who received the $10,000 for a Lincoln statue, is a young girl of about twenty who has been studying her art for a few months, never made a statue, has some plaster busts on exhibition, including her own. . . . has a pretty face, long dark curls and plenty of them, wears a jockey hat and a good deal of jewelry, sees members at their lodgings or in the reception room at the Capitol, urges her claims fluently and confidently, sits in the galleries in a conspicuous position and in her most bewitching dress, while those claims are being discussed on the floor, and nods and smiles as a member rises and delivers his opinion on the merits of the case with the air of a man sitting for his picture, and so she carries the day over Powers, Crawford and Hosmer, and who not?

This story was carried in many other newspapers.

Strangely enough, Harriet Hosmer, Mrs. Swisshelm's particular protégée, seems to have admired Vinnie, as is proved by a pleasant letter bearing her signature now with Vinnie's personal papers in the Library of Congress.

Harriet's friend, Grace Greenwood, the writer, was not so generous, for she had desired the Lincoln commission for her own sister, Mrs. Ames.

A Connecticut writer, Ann S. Stephens reputed to "possess powers of description of the first order" was another of Vinnie's most vehement enemies.

However, nobody stirred up such a storm in a teacup as Mrs. Swisshelm, whom even the New York *Times* saw fit to call the *Dragon of the Hesperides*, for "she seems to be too hard on that child of genius, Miss Vinnie Ream."

The same newspaper on July 28, 1866, had described Vinnie as "young and fascinating."

Vinnie's own personal dragon, Mrs. Swisshelm, was outraged. Her temper did not improve when the St. Louis *Evening News* bluntly described her as "Mrs. Swisshelm, who dearly loved to crucify a sister," further criticizing her "bitter pen."

This newspaper confessed to having been somewhat influenced by such a well-established columnist as Mrs. Swisshelm, especially when she accused the pretty sculptress of lobbying in order to obtain the coveted commission. After they had sent a correspondent to "investigate" both Vinnie and her work, they were completely won over by her surprising skill and her integrity. The correspondent wrote:

> We confess to having been to some extent unfavorably impressed by these adverse criticisms, and can therefore with the more candor say that an inspection of what she has accomplished and a knowledge of the unpropitious circumstances under which she has worked, has caused us to reverse our judgment and has inspired a very hearty admiration of the heroism with which this young girl has labored on uncomplainingly in the way her genius prompted, under perhaps the most chilling and discouraging influences that ever a youthful artist encountered. The modicum of truth in the harsh criticism above quoted is that Miss Ream has a pleasing face, which may be a serious drawback for an artist but which is no fault of hers and which is certainly the least of the gifts she has in mind. Of any trace of vanity, frivolity or giddiness she shows nothing whatever. She seems in fact to think of nothing but her art, having that unbounded enthusiasm in it and love

for it that leaves no room for trivialities. The facts we hear, from those who have watched her career, of the devotion she gives to her art, and the indefatigable assiduity with which she seizes every opportunity to perfect herself in it, remind one of the circumstances of the early career of another self-cultivated artist of the same sex, Rosa Bonheur.

Vinnie had no objection to being classed with Rosa Bonheur, that most successful painter of horse fairs, but she had no desire to copy her mode of working dress—a "daring" knickerbocker suit. She preferred to engage in sculpture wearing a rough smock, large apron, and old school shoes with rubber toes.

When the Cincinnati *Chronicle* announced that "Vinnie Ream is said to be a handsome likeness of the picture of Madame de Staël" this was much more to Vinnie's own romantic taste. Not every girl was compared with that intellectual creature who had been exiled by Napoleon for spiritedly opposing him!

A Washington matron named Mrs. Calhoun wrote to the New York *Tribune* a criticism of Vinnie, whom she described as "coarse, spiteful and injurious." She insisted that Vinnie "ran amuk" in Washington. Her letter antagonized readers so much that the newspaper afterward insisted in print:

> We cannot imagine why anybody but Mrs. Swisshelm (they wisely refrained from mention of their own spleen-filled reader's letter) should oppose the appropriation voted by Congress to Miss Vinnie Ream for a statue of the late President Lincoln.

. . . Why not let this promising artist peacefully enjoy the opportunity extended to her for studying art at Rome and for developing the genius which she is said to possess?

Much to her satisfaction, Vinnie had the last laugh on the ungenerous Mrs. Calhoun, for none other than Horace Greeley, founder and editor of this same New York *Tribune*, commissioned "Little Vin" as he called her, to "sculp my bust"!

❧ 7 ❧

THE FAIRY QUEEN

I F VINNIE REAM had a personal dragon, she also found herself a fairy queen.

Mrs. Elizabeth Cady Stanton, mentioned in Phebe A. Hannaford's *Daughters of America* as having been "quoted, ridiculed and abused into a national fame," was by occupation a lady reformer, writer, lecturer, and temperance worker. She often declared that "she would willingly give her body to be burned for the sake of seeing her sex enfranchised" although she was certainly the most enfranchised female of her generation. So great was her fervor that she only consented to marry on the condition that she be allowed to spend her honeymoon attending an anti-slavery convention in London. Seven children were born of this amazing union with the plucky Mr. Stanton. The children, like their insignificant father, Mrs. Stanton ruled with a rod of iron, which they do not seem to have minded, for they always lovingly spoke of her as their "Fairy Queen."

Said to have addressed the New York State Legislature more than any other woman, "Lizzie," as the members fondly called her, found herself asked on more than one occasion, *"Who is Vinnie Ream?"* Sensing an able recruit in the fight for women's rights, the "Fairy Queen"—carrying a black parasol for her scepter—marched upon Washington.

Mrs. Stanton had little difficulty in locating Vinnie's studio, for it was a popular rendezvous for Washington residents and visitors wishing to see the "notorious" girl sculptor at work on the plaster figure of Lincoln. Never did any sculptor work so publicly or before so many critical eyes.

Upon arrival, the "Fairy Queen" noted approvingly that in spite of her working outfit Vinnie Ream was a particularly pleasing specimen of femininity. The little studio had been considerably brightened by copies of works of art that Vinnie had hung around the walls. A fire burned cheerfully in the grate, while in the window hung three cages containing several canaries and other singing birds. A white dove perched happily upon one of the sculptress's shoulders. With her hair falling carelessly down her back, Vinnie appeared to the formidable Mrs. Stanton at that first meeting as "a mature Botticelli cherub." This was not such an astounding observation, for the "cherub" even had a harp, loaned to her by an adoring gentleman admirer. It stood framed by two wire-tiered stands filled with miniature potted palms.

Mrs. Stanton announced who she was, being in turn cordially greeted by Vinnie. Everyone knew of Lizzie Stanton, who could be a good friend to an ambitious young woman—or a formidable enemy.

Flashing a benevolent smile, the "Fairy Queen" fished in her large carpetbag to produce what appeared to be a scroll. This she pressed firmly into Vinnie's plaster-daubed hands.

"Child," she declared, "we wish your name here."

The tone of voice sounded to Vinnie more like a command than a wish. She took the scroll, unrolled the end, and read the startling title:

A Plan to Move on the Works of Man, the Monster.

Vinnie choked on the words, for several of the gentlemen mentioned underneath by name were those who had befriended her in the past.

"Oh no, Mrs. Stanton!" she bravely exclaimed. "I will not sign this." Rolling it up, she thrust the offending missive back into Lizzie's carpetbag. "I don't wish publicity, and I am not of your thinking on this question."

Lizzie's mouth opened and shut with surprise. She was used to such determined outbursts from members of the male opposition, but not from a slip of a girl. Her own daughters would not dare to address her like that. She was tempted to give Vinnie a good shaking, but Vinnie was adamant.

"But it enters into your interests. It concerns the recognition of woman, and woman's labor under the government." Lizzie Stanton sank into a Gothic-styled chair. She was excited and out of breath.

Vinnie stood her ground like a bantam before a formidable rooster. "I am not a woman's rights advocate, ma'am." Her voice was calm but firm.

"Why, child," cried Mrs. Stanton, "you are a working girl, getting your bread by your hands. If you do not help yourself and us, how can woman help you?"

Vinnie breathed hard. "Mrs. Stanton," she replied, her voice bitter, "no help has any woman ever given me here. From Grace Greenwood to Mrs. Swisshelm, they have all sought to strike me down. Mrs. Calhoun writes to the *Tribune* that she has not seen any of my work, but that she knows it is bad. All of them can find no larger occupation than attacking a poor girl, and their venom—" she said the words contemptuously "—has extended to personal canvassing against me. No, madam! Driven out of any desire for their patronage and co-operation, I will be befriended by gentlemen only; for whilst I never got any justice from a woman, I was never treated meanly by a man."

"I know Mrs. Swisshelm," said Mrs. Stanton. "She is a friend of mine, and prominent in the movement."

Vinnie looked for the moment like an angry child. "I forbear to enumerate the many malignant, vulgar and unprovoked things she wrote against me and had published," she said, her eyes filling with tears, "though I will not say they did not wound me to the heart. Then they were sent to me and to my friends." Vinnie produced a handkerchief from the pocket of her smock and blew her nose. "They aimed higher than my profession—at my character and my life."

The "Fairy Queen" was impressed, for the girl before her spoke with conviction and honesty. Besides, she hated to see another woman cry. "Grace Greenwood also wrote against you?" she asked, for she knew Grace very well and did not wish to believe ill of her.

"Yes, madam. In the *Advance* she upbraided my patrons and called me a child. She asked Congress to pay my school bills but to take me away from sculpture, adding that if any work was to be given out, it should be given to that Roman matron, Mrs. Ames—and Mrs. Ames is Grace Greenwood's sister."

Lizzie made no comment, for the words, poured out with such innocent intensity by the angelic-looking girl before her, had found their mark. Nonplussed, she tried to change the subject.

"Mrs. Stephens [Ann S. Stephens] was no more considerate?"

Vinnie drew her small figure up to its full height. "She, madam, not only talked against me—a stranger to her—wherever she could get a group to listen, but she made a personal visit to Thaddeus Stevens [a dominating figure in Congress] begging him to take away my studio!

" 'What is she doing ill?' Mr. Stevens asked." Here Vinnie gesticulated with her hands. "Mrs. Stephens replied, 'Decorating her studio with flowers, wearing long hair, attracting the men, and thereby lobbying.'

" 'Well,' said Mr. Stevens, 'it seems to me that you are round here lobbying a good deal, Mrs. Stephens, if talking to Congressmen is lobbying. I have never seen Miss Ream at all.'

"So he took up his crutch, hobbled over to see me, befriended me immediately and boldly."

This time it was the "Fairy Queen" who blew her nose. Oh, she thought, what a splendid orator this Vinnie Ream would make for the glorious cause.

However, Vinnie hadn't finished. "Mrs. Stanton," she concluded, "the men have more heart for my sex than the women. Their jealousy is at least [as] large as [their] emulation. Repelled by wrongs in the way I have stated, I was compelled to learn the generosity of men, and I do not regret the lesson."

With this, Vinnie returned to her unfinished statue of Abraham Lincoln.

Quietly, Lizzie Stanton rose to go, her petition to ban "Man the Monster" still unsigned. In her favor, let it be said that she afterward always spoke well of the mature cherub by whom she had been vanquished.

❧ 8 ❧

BEAUTY AND THE BEAST

I am not given to writing of the people whom I
meet, especially those of my own sex—I am not a
"man and a brick"—but I have been so charmed
with the lovely young sculptor, Miss Ream, that I
cannot forbear speaking of her here. Publicity she
cannot avoid, for her fame is thrust upon her. Her
genius will not permit her to tread the retired path
that woman naturally prefers, so I trust I shall be
pardoned for recording my admiration. . . .

She is entirely unspoiled and free from affectation.
She darts in and out of the studios here, illuminat-
ing them like a stray sunbeam, and looking like one
of her own beautiful statues into which some mod-
ern Pygmalion has breathed the breath of life. Her
modest estimate of herself, her earnest enthusiasm
and poetic temperament, her devotion to her art,
her fine spirits combined with real good sense and
much cultivation—for she has read books to some
purpose—make up a most interesting and attractive
character, and in her future career hosts of friends
will watch her with interest and pride.

So a Southern belle wrote of Vinnie in a letter to the
Louisville *Courier.* She had been one of the scores of critical visitors who had sought out Washington's most popular
tourist attraction—Miss Vinnie Ream at work on the pre-
liminary plaster statue of Abraham Lincoln. At times, the
demand to see Vinnie's small basement studio in the old

part of the Capitol building became so great that she was obliged to limit the flow of admirers and detractors. When a correspondent for the New York *Times* arrived for an "audience," a small enamel card pinned to the door announced, NO ADMISSION UNTIL 2 P.M. Nevertheless, he found "the witching little artiste in her linsey-woolsey working gown" to have "a warm heart." In his story, published January 19, 1867, he notes her "tiny, pink fingers," "long raven lashes," "bright black eyes," and "long dark curls and plenty of them." So well did Vinnie impress him that he later described the offending Mrs. Swisshelm as being "maddened with bitter envy."

Most artists would have withered under the scrutiny of so varied a selection of visitors, but Vinnie was not of the wilting kind. Not least among the visitors were the young gentlemen callers, generally armed with bouquets of flowers (wax ones in winter), with their flattering proposals of matrimony. One by one she sent them away. Her fame traveled far, so that some proposals arrived by mail. Even Brigham Young, the Mormon leader, desired her for one of his wives, an invitation that Vinnie "diplomatically and respectfully declined."

Another rejected suitor, more energetic than the others, expressed his thoughts in verse:

> She has a lover for each curl
> That decks her pretty brow!

At this important stage of her career she was more interested in the completion of her statue than in contemplating matrimony. Her sister Mary had made a promising marriage to a man much older than herself, wealthy Major Perry Fuller, and her brother Bob, mustered out of the Confederate cavalry, had married a beautiful Chickasaw Indian girl named Anna Guy. Through mutual friends Vinnie heard news of Boudy, the man who up to that time had meant most in her own life. He was playing a leading role in restoring peaceful relations between the Cherokees and the United States. Boudy had started his own tobacco factory in the Indian Territory, but this was to be seized by the government in 1868.

Vinnie had never lost contact with John Ridge, maintaining a regular correspondence with him. He had not been in good health for sometime. Just before his premature death in 1868, he had sent her his photograph, in which he was wearing a fashionable pair of checkered trousers. John, like Boudy, belonged to her youth, yet in spite of Vinnie's immature years they had always treated her as a grownup. When John died, she knew that someone who had truly believed in her capabilities had passed from her life. This only increased the incentive to prove that he had been right.

Working on a government commission was often nerve-racking, for even when she had completed the plaster figure she knew that it might not be satisfactory. When the model was finished, it was to be submitted for approval or disapproval to the Secretary of the Interior. Under oath, as part of his public duty, he was to determine whether at that stage the work was worthy of the late, beloved President.

With all the daily interruptions, progress seemed slow, even with Vinnie's quick fingers. Besides, one could hardly shut out those very citizens of the United States whose money would in the end, she hoped, pay for her long hours of labor. Not one cent of the initial half of the ten thousand dollars promised her was to be paid until the full-length plaster model was finally approved.

"All this work," thought Vinnie, "and they may not even like it."

When the model was finished to the satisfaction of the Secretary of the Interior, the next step would be for Vinnie to see it safely across the ocean to Italy, where it would be copied in the best Carrara marble.

Her method of approach to her work was unique, for she had first modeled the statue without "drapery," inviting the prominent surgeons of the city in to examine its anatomical proportions. Thus assured as to their correctness, she began to "dress" Mr. Lincoln, making sure that he had "comfortable" shoes for his "large feet." Unlike the artist who had portrayed George Washington barelegged in a Roman toga, Vinnie decided that Lincoln should be given "a realistic truly American" appearance.

Recalling Mrs. Lincoln's kindness to her when she was modeling the late President's head at the White House, Vinnie wrote, out of courtesy and respect, soliciting her help in securing a faithful likeness of the President in the monumental task ahead. Unfortunately for the young sculptress, Mrs. Lincoln, in her crazed state of grief, refused even to remember her. By a strange coincidence, the former First Lady was an intimate friend of Vinnie's arch-enemy, Jane Grey Swisshelm, "Dragon of the Hesperides."

Cruelly dwelling upon Vinnie's humble origin (although Lincoln had also been born in a log cabin), Mrs. Lincoln states "In *your* case, your home was far removed from ours in Washington."

The text of her letter reads:

Chicago,
Sept. 10th 66.

Miss Vinnie Ream,

Your letter has been received and I hasten to return an early reply. I shall be unable to comply with your request and you will allow me to say you are undertaking a very sacred work, one of great responsibility, which artists of world-wide renown would shrink from, as incapable of the great task. Every man, woman and child in our land felt as if they knew my beloved and illustrious husband, even if they had seen him but once. In *your* case, your home was far removed from ours in Washington, even *if* you visited there, during the late President's administration. With his life of toil, he had no opportunities and *far less* inclination, to cultivate the acquaintance of any save those who were compelled to be with him daily in saving our great nation from the hands of its enemies.

As every friend my husband knew was familiar to me, and as your name was not on the list, consequently you could not have become familiar with the expression of his face, which was so variable, even to those and especially myself, who had passed almost a life time in studying its changes. The photographs that abound in the country have never done justice to my dear husband, yet I will admit, if you had *even* been introduced to him in the gaping crowd, the kind and beautiful expression of his countenance would never have been forgotten.

That happiness was mine for long years of greater felicity, than is usually allotted to frail humanity and his expression was so changing, yet always so kind and almost heavenly—that with my heart *then* as *now*, filled with unutterable love for him who so truly and fervently returned it—I cannot fix my distressed mind—on any particular look, hence the difficulty of the task for *you*, a stranger to this great, good and Christ-like man.

Praying that you may have success,

I remain,

Truly,

MARY TODD LINCOLN

But interruptions and critical harassments to her work were small beside the qualms Vinnie suffered when, overnight, she became involved in the unprecedented impeachment proceedings brought by the powerful Radical Republicans against the new President, Andrew Johnson, a native of North Carolina and the son of a shoemaker. Johnson's endeavor to carry out Lincoln's ideas for reconciliation with the South appalled and incensed them, for up to that time they had believed "honest and forthright" Andrew Johnson to be their man. Johnson, however, was not the man to be intimidated, even when accused unjustly of "usurpation of the law, corrupt use of the veto power, interference at elections, and misdemeanors."

Positive of enough votes to convict Johnson of the charges, the Radicals picked one of their own number, Benjamin F. Wade, to be President *pro tempore* of the Senate, for the man holding that office would automatically become President of the United States should Johnson be found guilty. Somewhat prematurely, Wade even picked his own Cabinet!

The impeachers were disturbed when their private detective, whose job it was to spy upon possible defectors, discovered that a Radical member from Kansas, Senator Edmund Gibson Ross, was seriously thinking of voting for Johnson's acquittal. The loss of Ross's vote might well foil their plans to destroy the President. *This was the same Senator Ross who was a boarder in Vinnie's home.*

Ross and six other wavering impeachers met secretly in Vinnie's little studio in the Capitol. While history was being made, Vinnie served green tea brewed in her "highly polished" brass kettle with the lighted spirit lamp underneath. On occasion, she even interrupted their arguments to voice her own opinions. She is credited as having advised Ross to vote for the President's acquittal, because she believed Johnson to be "good and great."

General Daniel Sickles was sent by the impeachers to the Ream home to reason with Senator Ross, but word of his pending visit reached the ears of the President's men. Knowing the General to be a ladies' man, they asked Vinnie to intercept him on the street while Ross "escaped" to the home of a friend.

Vinnie, ever the enchantress, delighted the General so much by her witty conversation that by the time they eventually reached her home, Ross was gone.

When the story leaked out next day, Sickles was the subject of much ridicule in Washington. For her part, Vinnie became the victim of persecution at the hands of the Radicals, who did their best to frighten the girl into influencing Senator Ross to vote against the President. After all, was she not Ross's protégée? Surely he had helped her achieve the Lincoln statue commission. If she could charm one elderly man into forgetting his mission, as she had done General Sickles, she could successfully apply her powers of persuasion to Senator Ross.

If she did not help them, she was bluntly told, her studio would be taken away and the precious plaster cast for the Lincoln statue ruined.

It was a terrible predicament for a young woman. By refusing to influence Ross, Vinnie knew she would probably lose not only the ten thousand dollars, but all chance of subsequent fame as well. To her credit, like President Johnson, she refused to be intimidated, declaring that her personal opinion of Senator Ross was far too high to attempt to influence him in any way. Secretly, she also believed the President to be innocent. Even when a politician-author bearing so formidable a name as George Washington Julian was sent to tell her that if she did not mend her ways and help the impeachers she would be "ruined," Vinnie—though trembling visibly—held fast to her ideals. Playing for time, she informed him that she knew nothing of Senator Ross's plans, "innocently" asking "as he is a good Republican will he surely not vote for the conviction of the President?"

George Washington Julian had come to vanquish, not to be vanquished! Yet he was still muttering incoherently when Vinnie gently pushed him out of her studio.

On the night prior to the impeachment vote, General Sickles was again sent to the Reams's house, where he was informed by Vinnie's mother that Senator Ross was not at home. The General announced that this time he would stay all night if necessary. When Mrs. Ream protested, he sat down on the best red-plush sofa. He had a long wait as, forewarned, Senator Ross slept at the home of a friend.

Vinnie's harassment during these worrying days is amplified in an article entitled "Beauty and the Beast." It appeared June 19, 1868, in the Liberty *Tribune* (Missouri). Of course, Vinnie was Beauty; the beast was Benjamin Franklin Butler, a House manager for the impeachment and a gentleman whom the Good Lord had failed to bless with good looks. In fact, Butler had a practically bald head, heavy-lidded slit eyes, and a short walrus mustache similar to a Chinese mandarin's.

The article said:

> She is almost a child in years, but a braver or more aspiring enthusiast never lived. Her endeavors to perfect herself have been from the first arduous and

unintermitted. She was singled out by the dishonored men who were at the head of the impeachment as a victim, because, as ridiculously alleged, Miss Ream "influenced" the vote of a Senator for the acquittal of the President. Mr. Ross is a gentleman whose family, consisting of a wife and several children, resides at his home in Kansas. Sent here to Washington to represent that state in the Senate, Mr. Ross applied for and has since occupied rooms at the home of his old acquaintance and neighbor in Kansas, Robert L. Ream.

The piece concluded upon a highly sentimental note so loved by writers of that era, maintaining that if Little Vin were deprived of her studio, the model for Lincoln's statue would "shrink, and crack to pieces . . . There would be nothing left save a shattered, shapeless mass, to be moistened, after it is too late, by a young girl's tears."

9

AND SO TO ROME

ON MAY 26, 1868, Vinnie Ream had the satisfaction of seeing President Andrew Johnson acquitted of the impeachment charges against him. Thirty-five Senators had voted in favor of conviction against nineteen for acquittal. Johnson was actually saved by only one vote, a two-thirds vote being necessary for conviction.

Vinnie's friend, Senator Ross, paid dearly for his courageous refusal to vote against the President. His political career was ruined, and at the end of his Senatorial term, along with the other six dissenters, he retired from office. As for Vinnie, her ninety-odd pounds felt the full fury of the defeated Radical Republicans. She was told to vacate her studio forever.

Instead of complying, Vinnie hurried off to find Congressman Thaddeus Stevens, whose portrait bust she had made and who had once taken her side against Ann S. Stephens, the writer. Often referred to as "the most powerful man in the political life of the nation," Stevens had a terrifying personality. His long thin face was ashen white; his head was topped with a dark brown wig. He had ferocious, beetling eyebrows and a club foot. To the end of his life, he was carried to his usual seat in the House, his features "scarred by the crooked autograph of pain."

Thaddeus Stevens, a dying man when Vinnie appealed for his help, was bitterly disappointed over the Johnson acquittal. Notwithstanding, he was still Vinnie's friend. Furious that she, a woman, should be made the victim of such unjust punishment, he exerted his influence on her behalf. This resulted in Vinnie's being allowed to keep her studio in the Capitol building. Thanks to Stevens, the precious plaster statue, now almost finished, was saved from possible destruction.

At last it was ready for the all-important inspection of the Honorable O. H. Browning of Illinois, who had succeeded James Harlan as Secretary of the Interior. He had not met Vinnie previously, his predecessor having signed the order commissioning the work. Vinnie waited in nervous anticipation for his verdict.

By extreme good fortune, nobody was more competent to judge her efforts than Browning, as he had been Lincoln's close friend for more than a quarter of a century. A cultured man and a lover of the arts, he would have dismissed any representation of the late President that was not of the highest workmanship or quality. Warmly and emphatically, he pronounced himself pleased with Vinnie's "highly creditable" workmanship. The first payment of five thousand dollars was made!

The newspaper columns sang Vinnie's praise, so that even jealous critics like the "Dragon of the Hesperides" were forced to retreat behind paragraphs of excuses. "Sheer fabrication," ranted the "Dragon" to the editors of the Missouri *Democrat* in a public letter dated January 16,

1869, "so far as it details my personal interference in Miss Ream's affairs." Even so, Mrs. Swisshelm threw one final barb. "So, Miss Vinnie [at least she now knew her first name was not Minnie] must be reduced to straits for a crown of martyrdom, with which to purchase enough of the public money to carry her to Rome, when she placed me at the head of her list of persecutors."

The *Evening News*, St. Louis, voiced the general opinion of all those who had viewed the completed plaster model of Vinnie's "dear Mr. Lincoln."

Her design for the Lincoln statue will serve as a test of her ability to model a satisfactory statue of Mr. Lincoln. It has been said in Congress and elsewhere that it was beyond the ability of her girlish hand to deal with such a subject—that it "needed the masculine grasp," etc., etc. Well, a good many artists of the male persuasion have grappled with it during the past year, and the result has been the turning out of Mr. Lincoln in almost every conceivable style. We have him striking a Napoleonic attitude, with distended eye and arms crossed over a protuberant breast. We have him glowering, with Forrestian air, [Edwin Forrest, the actor] at a set of broken handcuffs. We have him pointing with melodramatic swagger to an axe and rail. We have him in Roman toga, very much to the disadvantage of his lank figure. We have him in bulging trousers, a smart cloak, and with his strongly-marked grotesque features so idealized as to pass for a Byron. We have him holding all sorts of documents at all sorts of angles, sometimes poised on his left leg and sometimes on his right. The masculine grapplers seem to have about exhausted themselves, and the result is not so decisive as to exclude competition. Suppose we give the feminine grasp a show. Her model is yet in the rough, but it shows points of excellence that promise well. The attitude is Lincolnian, and the artist, who made her study from life, has succeeded in catching the benign expression of face that should be perpetuated in a statue of Mr. Lincoln.

In June, 1869, accompanied by her parents and two pet doves, Vinnie set sail for France en route to Rome. With her precious Lincoln model safe in the hold of the ship, she took some well-earned relaxation. During the voyage, she charmed both fellow passengers and the captain with her songs, accompanying herself on a guitar. Having seen the plaster model safely landed at Le Havre, from where it would be sent to Rome, Vinnie set off to search Europe.

In Paris, she studied for a time under Léon Joseph Florentin Bonnat (1833-1932), a French portrait painter whose reputation had been recently established by his graphic religious painting entitled "St. Vincent de Paul taking the place of a Galley Slave."

It was Bonnat who introduced her to Gustave Doré (1833-1883), French artist and sculptor whose full name was Louis Christophe Paul Gustave Doré. Today, he is mostly remembered for his illustrations of books by such authors as Rabelais and Balzac. During his lifetime he was said to have "caught much of the authors' spirit," although at times the critics found his drawings somewhat "weird and horrible." Gustave Doré enjoyed knowing Vinnie so much that he dedicated to her a drawing of Judith holding up the lifeless head of Holofernes, the Assyrian commander —a strange choice of subject for dedication to "an uncomplicated American girl."

Doré gladly consented to Vinnie's request to model a portrait bust of him. So did the controversial Père Hyacinthe, which was the monastic name of Charles Loyson, who once had attracted great crowds as a preacher at St. Sulpice in Paris. He had entered the Carmelite order in 1862, from which he had been excommunicated the year before he met Vinnie "for persisting in denouncing (what he termed) the abuses of the church." Like many men, he proposed marriage to Vinnie, an offer she promptly refused.

Under somewhat unique circumstances, it was also in Paris that Vinnie bought her first harp. Ever since the Sisters in the Washington convent had first introduced Vinnie to this particular musical instrument, it had remained her favorite. Her long-time ambition had been to own a harp of fine craftsmanship, but such instruments were expensive and hard to find.

By sheer chance, Vinnie heard of a countess whose possessions were being seized by creditors. The unfortunate woman owned a splendid harp so, escorted by the American ambassador, Vinnie lost no time in calling upon the countess. Moved by her story, Vinnie purchased the harp for considerably more than it was worth.

Furnished with a letter of introduction to prominent residents of the Holy City by no less a personage than William H. Seward, Secretary of State under Abraham Lincoln, Vinnie finally arrived in Rome, where she took a studio and house at Number 45, Via de San Basilio. "She visits Europe with a view to the more successful prosecution of the work with which she has been entrusted," Seward had written.

There was a flourishing colony of Americans living in Rome, including the famous painter George Peter Alexander Healy (1813-1894), to whom Vinnie carried a letter of introduction written by Senator Lyman Trumbull of Illinois, one of the seven Republicans who had voted against President Johnson's conviction.

Vinnie loved Rome right from the beginning. The feeling that she walked always on historic ground pleased her. Treated courteously by celebrities, statesmen, and fellow artists of other nationalities, Vinnie was equally welcomed by the Italians, although they never became used to the cups of tea that she dispensed in her studio instead of the customary red wine. Vinnie had served tea to Senators in Washington and saw no reason to change her way.

Her beauty attracted as many as twenty love-stricken beaus a day, all ready with flowery offerings, to ask for her hand in marriage. Vinnie, an old hand at dealing with gentlemen callers, poured each a cup of tea, allowed him time to drink it, and then sent him home. Generally, they were back the next afternoon to try again, their gifts of flowers making her studio look like a florist's shop. Each morning, often pursued by a male guard, Vinnie set out for her walk along the Via Gregoriana where the view was truly panoramic, encompassing as it did the gigantic dome of St. Peter's Basilica, the historic Castel Sant'Angelo, together with a vast expanse of open *campagna*. The Quirinal palace with its gardens of flowering ilex and magnolias, the impressive tower of the Capitol, the low rounded dome of the Pantheon, and the rugged gray shell of the Colosseum were all included in the picture that delighted her artist's eyes. Small humplike mounds crowned with umbrella trees and tall feathery cypresses might well have formed the background of a medieval painting. Over everything hung a canopy of cloudless blue.

Lavinia and Robert Ream settled happily into their life in Rome. Their penurious days of keeping a Washington boarding house were behind them; Vinnie had assumed full responsibility for their support. Her concern for her parents' welfare during their Roman stay was noted, in their letters home, by several fellow Americans. The Italians, with their great reverence for old age, noticed it also.

Before making her intended trip to the quarries of Carrara to select the marble from which the Lincoln statue would be carved, she studied with Luigi Majoli, the prominent Italian sculptor. Once, in the course of conversation, she told him of her wish to make a bust of the formidable Cardinal Antonelli, whom most people held in awe. Born in the village of Sonnino, in 1806, Giacoma Antonelli was the son of a woodcutter. After a brilliant career in the Grand Seminary at Rome, Pope Gregory XVI gave him various ecclesiastical appointments. In 1847, Pope Pius IX had him made a cardinal and, in 1848, President of the liberal cabinet which drew up the *Statuto* or Constitution.

On the fall of the ministry, he fled with the Pope to Gaeta. Upon their return in 1850, he again became the Pope's chief minister.

Majoli could give Vinnie little encouragement, for the Cardinal was no easy man to deal with. Undaunted, Vinnie made herself a long white gown, then, demurely carrying a dove on either shoulder, requested an audience. The Cardinal was obviously moved at the sight of such a picture of innocence, for upon hearing the story of her life, he immediately agreed to the sittings. The result must also have pleased him, for he presented her with three large cameo medallions richly set in Etruscan gold. One depicted the head of Christ; the second, the Madonna cut from a ruby; and the third, a saint.

With the cameos came a card neatly inscribed:

> Card. Antonelli
> to his little friend
> Miss Vinnie Ream.
> Vatican, 1870.

Luigi Majoli could hardly believe his eyes when he saw them!

Wearing one of the Cardinal's cameos, Vinnie sat for her portrait in oils by George Healy. They had in common the fact that Abraham Lincoln had in his lifetime posed for both of them. This portrait, showing Vinnie wearing a gay Italian peasant costume, now hangs in the Smithsonian Institution in Washington.

Vinnie's next "conquest" was Franz Liszt (1811-1886), the great Hungarian composer. While visiting Rome in

1864, the musician had been caught up by the mysticism of the Catholic Church and decided to embrace Holy Orders. He was made an *abbé*.

Abbé Liszt spent his days in Rome composing and teaching students who came from the far corners of the world. The Hungarian Cabinet created him a noble in 1871, with a handsome annual pension. In 1875, he became director of the Academy at Budapest.

Although Liszt praised her harp playing, and presented her with a piece of music which he had composed in her honor, strangely enough Vinnie left no written record of her visits to the aging composer. However, she did engrave her impressions in stone, and her portrait of the Abbé is filled with a sense of his compassion and nobility.

THE MARBLE CITY

It was Sunday afternoon in Carrara during the early fall of 1870. The Reams had arrived the previous evening from Pisa, whose famous leaning tower had particularly fascinated Robert Ream. The next morning, Vinnie had awakened to the sound of church bells. From her window she could see, down in the piazza, groups of men of all ages gossiping together before going to Mass. Beyond the town rose mysterious wooded hillsides that in turn were overshadowed by the snowy peaks of the Apennines.

Dressing quickly, she had joined her parents in a breakfast of sweet rolls washed down by the blackest of coffee. Then, leaving Lavinia to read her Bible, Vinnie, holding her father's arm, stepped into the Square, where immediately she became the object of many admiring glances from the younger men gathered there.

Father and daughter set off in the direction of the little thirteenth-century cathedral, whose weather-beaten façade seemed to beckon a welcome. Vinnie was so excited that Robert Ream had to request her to be more careful how she twirled her sunshade, lest she should poke his eye out.

They found the cathedral to be built of the marble for which the city was famous. The outside was covered with dozens of exquisite carvings of tiny animals, both grotesque and beautiful. Peeping inside, for a service was in progress, they were entranced by the beauty of the rose window. The marble walls and pillars seemed darkened with the smoke of generations of candles.

The baptistry, containing two fonts—one for baptism by total immersion—particularly caught Vinnie's questing eye. The cover of the smaller font was composed of many different colored marbles—a Joseph's coat in stone! Robert Ream could hardly entice his daughter out into the sunshine again.

But now she was alone, having left her parents to rest in the comfortable hotel while she went for a walk in the hills above the town. Caught in a sudden shower, she was forced to take shelter in the mouth of an unused quarry and stood listening to the heavy rain drops pattering upon the rocks above her head. She had taken off her hat, turning it upside down to protect the sprays of pink roses and white daisies that covered the outside of the crown.

Spread out below her, clinging like a limpet to the hillside, was the little city of Carrara, famed for over hundreds of years for its marble. Beyond, stretched the blue sea. It seemed a dream that she was here at all, yet being Vinnie, the perfectionist, she had to see her task through in intimate detail. Nobody but she was going to choose the marble from which her statue of "dear Mr. Lincoln" was to be chiseled.

The parched hillside absorbed the rain like a sponge. Everything around Vinnie smelled fresh and clean. Picking up her skirt with one hand and holding her precious hat with the other, she was able at last to pick her way carefully down the sodden trail back to the city. Turning, she paused for a moment in admiration for those same mountains which, from time immemorial, had provided the marble that was the means of giving so much beauty to the world.

Although she knew only a smattering of Italian, Vinnie had little trouble in conversing about the marble trade, for there were several Americans and Englishmen in the little city engaged in some branch or other of the business. Luigi Majoli had recommended whom she should see about choosing the stone. First, however, she was determined to visit the quarries themselves. It was easy to find a marble dealer willing to take her, and her father also was delighted to accompany them.

This time, it was not raining when she set out with her little party. As they ascended one of the many pathways, the scenery in the valley below lay wild and unspoiled. It was Monday morning and the two boys engaged to carry their packs were delighted to earn a lira each, for up at the quarries they would have earned no more at a much more backbreaking task. They guided the party to a small lodging house in the mountains, known as a *locanda*, where the traditional bread, wine, and generous amounts of sausage were served. The crisp, cool air had given Vinnie a good appetite, so that she enjoyed her meal.

After lunch, they climbed on to where the roadway narrowed because of piles of marble debris that had caused minor landslides. The guides warned them all to beware of loose stones falling down the mountainside.

They were also told to keep clear of the great white oxen whose task it was to haul the huge marble blocks. These patient-looking creatures had gained a reputation for being dangerous. A particularly bad-tempered beast would have his sharp curving horn tips painted red or black, as a warning to strangers. Vinnie decided that too often the drivers were more savage than their beasts. She had plenty to say concerning the way they prodded the poor animals with sharply pointed goads.

It was an exciting journey, especially when they heard cries of warning from above that a gunpowder fuse was about to be ignited. Taking shelter, they waited, fingers pressed into ears, until all danger was past.

Some of the quarries, Vinnie was told, were located on the top of cliffs, the men from the city and adjoining villages walking each morning to work and staying eight hours or more. There were about six hundred quarries, employing some ten thousand men and stretching over a radius of nearly thirty miles. A number of quarries had been worked by the ancient Romans before the advent of Christ. In one disused tunnel, Vinnie was shown the marks of instruments used by the Romans.

Vinnie soon learned that comparatively few of the quarries provided the choicest marble for statuary. For the equivalent of ninety dollars, a guaranteed piece could be bought. Should a flaw later be found, a new piece would be furnished, free of cost, by the quarry. The first-class quarries from which marble for statuary was taken were almost all owned by one man, an Italian, whose income was said to be about one hundred and twenty thousand dollars a year. Lesser workings producing a second grade of marble provided the material for making tombstones, washstand tops, and paving slabs.

Upon reaching one of the cutting mills, the precious blocks of statuary marble were immediately placed under cover, as a protection from the weather.

On the way down from the quarries, Vinnie and her companions visited one of the mills, located upon the banks of a fast-running stream. Here, to the gentle splashing of the giant water wheel, they watched a huge marble block at least five feet in length, four in width, and seven in depth, sawed into smooth slabs of one-and-one-half-inch thickness.

Vinnie particularly noted the saw. Made up of long pieces of iron, toothless, and four inches in depth, it was hung with heavy weights. As it groaned backward and forward with its several blades, water and sand regularly dropped from above. The sand, Vinnie discovered, did the actual cutting, being forced by the iron into the marble. The sand that emerged from such treatment was too finely pulverized for a second using.

When she asked the friendly mill owner how long it took for a large block to be sawed through, he replied, "Sometimes a week." The thin slabs were then marked with the owner's initials and made ready for shipment to the buying showrooms in the city.

Later, in Carrara, Vinnie had the opportunity to visit several of the many studios to be found there. She enjoyed seeing what the sculptors were making; it varied from a graceful Venus to a grim sepulchral bust copied from a photograph. She spent all of one morning choosing the marble block from which "The Statue" was to be carved.

After all, as she confessed to her mother, "It is no small task shopping for the entire American nation!"

❧ I I ❧

AN ENCOUNTER ON A TRAIN

THE YOUNG Danish writer with the dark brown hair, closely trimmed beard, and grayish-green eyes so uncharacteristic of his nationality, sat moodily watching the countryside rush past. Georg Morris Cohen Brandes was traveling by train from Florence to Rome. Although still only twenty-eight years old, he was highly esteemed in the world of letters.

An authority on esthetics and the history of literature, he had already published such books as *Esthetic Studies, French Esthetics in Our Day*, and *Criticisms and Portraits*.

Years later, when he was old, Georg Brandes was often to recall that morning of October 11, 1870. He could even remember what he saw from his seat by the window:

> Vines twine round the fruit-trees; black pigs and their families make their appearance in tribes; the lake of Thrasymene, near which Hannibal defeated the Romans, spreads itself out before us.

Toward midday when the train reached Perugia, a girl, whom he judged to be "English or North American," entered the carriage. It was Vinnie Ream, carrying her guitar case which she flung carelessly up into the luggage net. Behind her, walked her parents. Georg noticed that the girl "with brown eyes and brown hair" carefully

79

selected seats for Robert and Lavinia Ream. As the carriage compartment was designed to hold forty-eight people, there was no crowding. After much joking and laughter, Mr. and Mrs. Ream finally settled down for their afternoon siesta, a habit they had acquired from the Italians.

Then Vinnie, oblivious of the admiring glances the Italian men were giving her, looked about to find herself a seat. At last, she settled down opposite the young Danish writer who, being naturally shy, pretended not to notice her, an omission that hurt Vinnie's vanity. For sometime neither spoke and, if it had been left to Brandes, probably never would have done so. Vinnie, on the other hand, could never be accused by anyone of shyness. Leaning forward, she asked him the time in Italian—a stock tourist phrase she had learned. The Dane replied in a quiet, disinterested voice; Vinnie shrugged her shoulders.

She tried again, this time in English. "You are Italian?" Although she had already half-guessed that he wasn't.

Georg Brandes felt the color flooding his pale cheeks. Sweeping a hand through his hair, he half-mumbled an answer.

Vinnie laughed aloud, which put him somewhat at ease. "I hardly know twenty words in Italian," she confessed.

This time it was Brandes' turn to smile. He was already intrigued by this friendly girl.

Encouraged, Vinnie lost no time in telling him something of her life story; of how she had been born out on the wild Indian frontier, of her ambition to become a sculptress and of all the trials and tribulations it had brought her. Brandes was particularly interested in her description of Lincoln and her visits to the White House.

By the time Vinnie had finished telling her personal history, they were obliged to change trains, the railway tracks having been broken up to prevent Italian troops from entering the Papal States, then a territory independent from the rest of Italy, ruled by the Pope. In 1860, the Papal States had lost vast areas to Sardinia, but with the help of France were able to keep their remaining lands intact. When Napoleon III of France was deposed in 1870, Victor Emmanuel of Italy marched to annex Rome, capital of the Papal States.

"I will stay with you," exclaimed Vinnie impulsively. "Promise you will travel to Rome with us."

Georg Morris Brandes stumbled over his reply. Not for all the money in the world would he have had it any other way.

Soon Vinnie's parents were settled upon the new train, while their daughter and her Danish friend sat some distance apart from them. This time it was Brandes who did most of the talking. (It was surprising, he later thought, how contented he felt in the American girl's company.) His lectures, he informed her, would soon be published under the title of *Principal Tendencies in the Literature of the Nineteenth Century*. Somewhat apprehensively, he wondered what their reception would be, having already received criticism in his homeland as a freethinker and radical.

Vinnie advised him, from personal experience, not to worry about criticism, for she had successfully overcome an army of Mrs. Swisshelms. So intently were they talking that Brandes failed to notice the interest a Danish couple ("a mediocre artist and his wife") were taking in them. In Brandes' words, "with national astonishment and curiosity [they] watched the evident intimacy between the young foreigner and myself, concerning which every Scandinavian in Rome was informed a few days later."

The bridge had been blown up at Monte Rotondo so the travelers had to leave the train again. This time, they were forced to walk some distance over bad roads. Brandes noted in his autobiography, "she kept a place for me by her side." He added with apparent satisfaction later, traveling by carriage, "Thus I drove for the first time over the Roman Campagna, by moonlight, with two brown eyes gazing into mine. I felt as though I had met one of Sir Walter Scott's heroines, and won her confidence at our first meeting."

It is doubtful if a Scott hero was ever expected to carry a guitar case and a large wicker cage containing two American-born white doves!

That romantic ride over the Campagna must likewise have pleased Vinnie, for Georg was invited to call next day at Number 45, Via de San Basilio. There he saw some of her work, and was much amused by the adept way she dismissed her gentleman callers. Sixteen handsome Italians arrived during his first afternoon visit, and left feeling somewhat disgruntled when they saw that he, a foreigner, was privileged to stay. While Vinnie put a finishing touch to her bust of Liszt, Georg arranged her gifts of flowers. He also helped answer correspondence, which he noted was filled with proposals "of matrimonial nature."

"Vinnie Ream was by no means a Scott heroine," he declared after a second visit, "but a genuine American, and doubly remarkable to me as being the first specimen of a young woman from the United States with whom I became acquainted."

Genuine American she might be, but Brandes mentioned in his outspoken way that he was not quite so impressed with her work as he was with her. For this reason he appealed to Vinnie, for she was very tired of having every young man praise her sculpture in order to gain her favors.

Wrote Brandes:

> Even after I had seen a good deal of her work, I could not feel wholly attracted by her talent, which sometimes expressed itself rather in a pictorial than a plastic form, and had a fondness for emotional effects. But she was a true artist, and a true woman, and I have never, in any woman, encountered a will like hers. She was uninterruptedly busy.

But not too busy to go walking with Georg Morris Brandes or to spend hours wandering in the great portrait galleries, her arm linked in his. The Spanish Steps, Michelangelo's *Pietà* under the massive dome of St. Peter's, and the mellowed walls of the Church of Saint Susannah—all these Vinnie visited with the handsome Dane. He even accompanied her when she went to sit for Mr. Healy, whom he called "the clever American painter."

But as a friend, Georg had limitations. When it came to his own particular field, he considered his knowledge superior to that of all others. Even Vinnie did not escape his criticism, as the following paragraph reveals:

> She was very ignorant of things outside her own field, and the words "my work" were the only ones that she spoke with passion. What she knew, she had acquired practically, through travel and association with a multiplicity of people. She hardly knew a dozen words of any language besides English, and was only acquainted with English and American writers; of poets, she knew Shakespeare and Byron best; from life and books she had extracted but few general opinions, but on the other hand, very individual personal views. These were based upon the theory that the lesser mind must always subordinate itself to the higher, and that the higher has a right to utilize freely the time and strength of the lesser, without being called to account for doing so. She herself was abjectly modest towards the artists she looked up to. Other people might all wait, come again, go away without a reply.

However, he did take the trouble to write Hans Brøchner, the Danish philosopher, a very complimentary letter concerning Vinnie and their first meeting—doves included!

Vinnie's opinion of Georg was just as outspoken—and probably only too true.

He confessed:

> Vinnie Ream's opinion of me was I was the most
> impolitic man that she had ever known. She meant,
> by that, that I was always falling out with people
> (for instance, I had at once offended the Danes in
> Rome by some sharp words about the wretched
> Danish papers), and in general made fewer friends
> and more enemies all the time. She herself won the
> affection of everyone she wished, and made every-
> one ready to spring to do her bidding. She pointed
> out to me how politic she had had to be over her
> art. When she had wished to become a sculptor,
> everyone in her native place had been shocked at
> the unfemininity of it, and people fabled behind
> her back about her depraved instincts. She, for her
> part, exerted no more strength than just enough to
> carry her point, let people talk as much as they liked,
> took no revenge on those who spread calumnies
> about her, showed the greatest kindliness even to-
> wards the evil-disposed, and so, she said, had not an
> enemy. There was in her a marvellous commingling
> of determination to progress rapidly, of self-restraint
> and of real good-heartedness.

We are also indebted to Georg for the following lively
picture of Vinnie:

> Rather small of stature, strong and healthy—she had
> never been ill, never taken medicine—with white
> teeth and red cheeks, quick in everything, when sev-
> eral people were present she spoke only little and
> absently, was cold, deliberate and composed as a
> man of strong character; but at the same time she
> was unsuspecting and generous, and in spite of her
> restlessness and her ambitious industry, ingratiat-
> ingly coquettish towards anyone whose affection she

wished to win. It was amusing to watch the manner in which she despatched the dutifully sighing Italians who scarcely crossed the threshold of her studio before they declared themselves. She replied to them with a superabundance of sound sense and dismissed them with a jest.

One day that I went to fetch her to the Casino Borghese, I found her dissolved in tears. One of the two beautiful doves who flew about the house and perched on her shoulders, and which she had brought with her from Washington, had disappeared in the night. At first I thought that her distress was half jest, but nothing could have been more real; she was beside herself with grief. I realized that if philologians have disputed as to how far Catullus' poem of the girl's grief over the dead sparrow were jest or earnest, it was because they had never seen a girl weep over a bird. Catullus, perhaps, makes fun a little of the grief, but the grief itself, in his poem, too, is serious enough.

Georg seems successfully to have held his own with Vinnie's persistent Italian suitors, although they could be a nuisance at times, such as the day when he was waiting to escort her to a fête. The important occasion was the anniversary of the death of Enrico Cairoli, one of the famous soldier brothers who had fallen in battle at Mentana. Just as Georg and Vinnie were about to leave for the festivities no less than twenty gentleman callers arrived. This was enough to upset any chosen escort, and Georg's feelings were not improved when he and Vinnie arrived late, to find the most interesting part of the fête over. Undaunted, Vinnie proposed they should go instead to the American chapel for "she must and would sing hymns."

Although a skeptic, Georg Brandes gallantly rose to the occasion, afterward admitting, somewhat grudgingly, that Vinnie "did sing them very well."

The chapel walls were bare of expensive ornamentation, being adorned with only the Ten Commandments and a few biblical texts. Over the small altar were painted the words: "Do This in Remembrance of Me."

As can be expected, Georg did not feel much at home. "I had to endure the hymns," he complained, "the sermon (awful), and the reading aloud of the Ten Commandments, with muttered protestations and Amens after each one from the reverent Americans."

Upon leaving the service Georg diplomatically said nothing, for he "did not know whether Vinnie might not be somewhat moved, for she sang at the end with great emotion." His tension was relieved, however, when, pinching his arm, she exclaimed, "That minister was the most stupid donkey I have ever heard in my life; but it is nice to sing."

As they walked through the busy streets Vinnie did most of the talking. Much to Georg's amusement, she critically analyzed the sermon, beginning with its text: "Thy sins are forgiven thee."

"What am I benefited if ever so many heavenly beings say to me: 'I pretend you have not done it,'" exclaimed Vinnie, "if I know that I have!"

Georg's ardent companionship proved no deterrent to Vinnie's work, for unlike many creative people she worked as successfully with an audience as without. While he sat patiently watching, she put the finishing touches to her great white statue of Abraham Lincoln. The marble she had picked with such care in Carrara was actually carved by one of the many skilled stonecutters who reproduced under her supervision the model made in clay and brought from America. This was the usual procedure adopted by other American sculptors and sculptresses, many of whom—unlike Vinnie—preferred to remain expatriates, never returning to their native country.

When Georg teased her about all the time he had "wasted" in her company, she became very serious. "People do not waste time with their friends," she answered so emphatically that Georg retorted, "What do I get from you?"

Laughing, Vinnie replied, "Inspiration."

"And that," Georg Brandes insisted many years later, "was the truth."

Yet their days together were all too short for, with the completion of the statue, Vinnie would be sailing home to deliver it. On October 20th she accompanied Georg to a gay Roman festival to celebrate the Italian army's triumphant entry into the city. The streets were hung with flags and bunting; gay spreads trailed from the iron balconies. Caught in the festive holiday spirit, Vinnie and Georg jostled their way through the boisterous, good-natured crowds. The night air was filled with the sound of music, crackling fireworks, and frantic cheering. From booths set up at the sides of the street, venders sold sizzling sausages cut from enormous rings. Italian girls ran to their windows to hold up candles and lamps.

During the last weeks of that memorable October, the two friends saw "the marvellous Northern Lights" together. Noting the occasion in his diary, Georg said:

> The northern half of the heavens, about nine o'clock in the evening, turned a flaming crimson, and white streaks traversed the red, against which the stars shone yellow, while every moment bluish flashes shot across the whole. When I discovered it I went to wake up the Reams' and fetched Vinnie down into the street to see it. It was an incredibly beautiful atmospheric phenomenon. Next evening it manifested itself on a background of black clouds, and that was the last beautiful sight upon which Vinnie and I looked together.

𑀉12𑀉

HOME AGAIN

V INNIE'S STUDIO at Number 45, Via de San Basilio was even more crowded than usual, the occasion being an important one. The Romans were being given a special viewing of the tall white statue of Abraham Lincoln. Other sculptors in the United States, some of them famous, had already produced figures of Lincoln for various civic institutions. Not one, however, had been responsible for a figure that had won universal acclaim.

From early morning a steady stream of visitors poured into the pleasant courtyard of the Reams' rented home. Dressed in white, with a large bow of brilliant green ribbon flowing from her waist, Vinnie stood happily beside her proud parents. In the background was Georg Brandes, for whom the occasion was tinged with sadness. Vinnie was leaving for home—a celebrity. They might never meet again.

Would fame and riches spoil the girl who so unabashedly had asked him to hold her two doves when they drove in an open carriage over the Roman *campagna*? Might not the spiteful attacks to which his writing was already being subjected embitter him as the years passed by? As he watched Vinnie accepting the countless bouquets of carnations and lilies from her admiring visitors, Georg Brandes felt the richer for having known her. Theirs had been an idyllic friendship. He would never forget it. "I am grateful to her," he declared in his diary. "She has communicated to me a something good and simple that one cannot see too much of and that one scarcely ever sees at all. . . . There was a certain deep note about all that her heart uttered. . . . She laughed when we read in the newspapers of Vinnie Ream, that, in spite of the ill-fame creative lady artists enjoy, far from being a monster with green eyes, she ventured to be beautiful."

There were still strangers viewing the statue when at the end of the day it was time for Vinnie and Georg to say good-bye. Perhaps it was a glimpse of what the busy future held for both of them, for neither would have any real privacy again. "Unfortunately a great many people were there," Georg afterward complained.

"I wish you everything good in the world," said Vinnie, clasping his hand, "and I know that you wish me the same."

And then, "Good-bye," Georg says. "A door opens, and a door closes, and people never meet again on this earth, never again, never—and human language has never been able to discover any distinction between good-bye for an hour, and good-bye forever.

"And now—no Roman elegy—" he declared, "I will hide her away in my memory." In a book Georg wrote Vinnie's epitaph:

Here lies
Vinnie Ream
Sculptor,
of Washington, U.S.A.
Six-and-twenty years of age.
This recollection of her is retained by
One who knew her
for seventeen days
and will never forget her.

Another friend in Rome who would miss Vinnie's personality was George Healy, the artist who had painted her portrait. All her life she carefully preserved his letter of appreciation:

> 54 Via Gregoriana
>
> My dear Miss Ream:
> Before you leave for our beloved country with your important national work which you have so successfully completed, I beg to tender you my sincere congratulations on the admirable likeness you have obtained in your statue of President Lincoln: it represents the very manner of our noble Patriot Martyr and will I feel sure give great satisfaction to our people when it is placed in the Capitol.
> I shall always remain under great obligations to Senator Trumbull for having made me acquainted with you, and be assured that your tender care of your father and mother has touched me very deeply.
> With the hope that you may have a safe and pleasant voyage, I remain, my dear young friend,
>
> Yours ever,
>
> GEO. P. A. HEALY.

Coming from such a distinguished artist, this was praise indeed!

Breaking their journey in London, the Reams were somewhat startled at the liberty taken by the London *Court Journal* which in an amazing story gives this description of Vinnie:

> She is a full-blooded Indian, very dark, but not ill-looking. She wears a single garment of linen cloth, which clings to her figure, and is merely confined about the waist by a scarf of blue gauze. Her hair is cut close in front and around her ears, then is left to flow upon her shoulders. A handkerchief of bright yellow silk is bound around her head, and is tied in a loose knot behind; her arms are bare to the shoulders and her ankles likewise, her naked feet being in richly embroidered moccasins.

During her short stay in London, Vinnie persuaded Dr. Charles Haddon Spurgeon (1834-1892), the great evangelical preacher, to sit for her while, to her intense gratification, she was invited to attend a reception given in her honor by the British government.

When she and her parents left England a friend presented her with a volume of Sir Walter Scott's poems. During the voyage, she read them over several times, the words of "The Coronach" lingering in her mind, and, later, to her mother's delight, she set them to music.

THE GREAT UNVEILING

THE ORDER OF ARRANGEMENTS
MADE BY THE
COMMITTEE ON PUBLIC BUILDINGS & GROUNDS
OF THE SENATE AND HOUSE OF REPRESENTATIVES
FOR
UNVEILING THE STATUE
OF THE LATE PRESIDENT LINCOLN,
Made by Miss Vinnie Ream,
to take place in the Rotunda of the Capitol,
on Wednesday Evening, January 25th,
at half-past seven o'clock, precisely.

VINNIE READ the official government announcement with mixed emotions, for what would happen if the American people did not like her representation of Mr. Lincoln?

In the roster of important personages who would attend the unveiling, Vinnie had actually been listed before President Ulysses Simpson Grant, Andrew Johnson's successor. For a girl born into a poor frontier family such an honor seemed a dream.

The official inspection of her statue, which had arrived undamaged from Rome, had taken place some days earlier. Describing the event, the Washington *Evening Star* reported on January 7, 1871:

> When it came time for the veil to be lifted there was
> a sudden hush in the buzz of conversation. . . . It

must have been an anxious moment to the courageous little sculptor and to her personal friends
present. Could it be that the fragile, youthful figure
standing there, pale and anxious, and rendered
more child-like in appearance by her petite form
and wealth of Dora-like curls, had made a success
where so many older sculptors—Brown notably and
recently—had failed? Was it possible that at her age,
and with her slight experience, she had made a
statue of Abraham Lincoln fit to be placed in the
Capitol of the nation? And then there was the formidable array of Illinoisians present, familiar with
the living Lincoln, and prompt to detect a defective
literal representation, however good the work might
be artistically. The veil was raised slowly, disclosing
first the base, bearing the simple words ABRAHAM
LINCOLN; then the well-remembered form; and
finally and essentially, the head of the Patriot Mar-
tyr. There was a momentary hush, and then an involuntary, warm, and universal demonstration of
applause gave the verdict of the distinguished and
critical gathering, and assured the artist that her
work was to be set down a success. There was another pause, while a more deliberate view was taken;
and then another, and another round of applause
confirmed and rendered final the involuntary de-
cision from the first impression. And then everybody
turned to where the little sculptor-girl stood, a little
in the rear with glad tears in her eyes, and congratu-
lations were poured in upon her from all quarters,
official and unofficial; the Illinoisians present being
foremost in expressing their satisfaction with her
representation of the man they revered. The expressed opinion of Senator Trumbull and others
from that State was that the statue gives that
thoughtful, benignant expression familiar to those

who knew Mr. Lincoln best, and which was best worth perpetuating in marble.

Even after such reassurance Vinnie was noticeably uneasy as, accompanied by a naturally proud Lavinia, she left for the official unveiling. Her father, whose health was failing, could not attend. They joined President Grant, Vicepresident Schuyler Colfax, General Sherman, Mayor Emery of Washington, Supreme Court Justices, members of the Committee of Arrangements, Senators, Cabinet members, foreign dignitaries, and prominent Naval officers at the unveiling.

President Grant greeted Vinnie kindly, telling her to be brave, for the general public would approve her work just as the Committee of Inspection had. Grant was well acquainted with the quality of Vinnie's sculpture, for she had modeled his head very successfully.

At a quarter after seven the distinguished group proceeded to the Rotunda where a platform had been erected, President Grant taking his place beside the Vice-president in the front row. Vinnie and Lavinia were seated two tiers behind them. It was bitterly cold in the vast Rotunda and Vinnie shivered visibly, although this was as much from nervous stress as from the freezing temperature.

Promptly at half-past seven the main doors, both east and west, were thrown open to admit the waiting crowd. Pushing and shoving people surged up the stairways, quickly filling whatever space remained behind the reserved seats. Outside, braving an icy wind and scattered snowflakes, the rest of the crowd pounded vainly against the doors that had now been shut against them. All through the ceremony their angry voices could be heard, while their fists sounded, according to Vinnie, "like roaring cannon."

Letting her eyes wander around the Rotunda walls, it seemed to Vinnie that all the patriots, warriors, statesmen, and explorers whose painted images adorned them were part of the huge throng there to honor Lincoln that night. Columbus, Penn, Washington, Adams, Franklin, De Soto, and the Pilgrim Fathers themselves gazed upon the sad, thoughtful face of Abraham Lincoln.

Over the great doorways were draped the national colors, while, ready to floodlight the statue at the proper time, was a newly-installed star fixture of gas jets. The huge swathed statue had been covered with a silk flag made by the weavers of Lyons in France; it bore the words:

Subscription populaire de la République Etats Unis offerte en mémoire d'Abraham Lincoln, Lyons, 1865.

The Marine band opened the evening's proceedings by playing a solemn dirge, after which Senator Justin Smith Morrill of Vermont, Chairman of the Committee of Arrangements, stepped to the front of the platform.

"Four years ago," he began, "a little girl from Wisconsin occupied a little place in the Post Office Department, at six hundred dollars a year. She had faith that she could do something better. Congress, with almost equal faith and liberality, gave her an order for the statue of the late deceased President Lincoln. That statue and the artist are now before you, and bespeak your sympathy."

At this point the audience, including President Grant, broke into loud applause. From her third-tier seat Vinnie bowed her head, color flooding her pale cheeks. A lump had formed in her throat, for even her mother was taking part in the heart-warming ovation. Seconds passed before Senator Morrill could conclude his brief speech by announcing: "Judge Davis, of the Supreme Court, will now unveil the statue."

Vinnie was weeping now, so quietly that only Lavinia noticed. Silently she took Vinnie's hand. Judge Davis slowly raised the flag, disclosing the tall lanky form of Mr. Lincoln. Round after round of spontaneous applause followed.

"They like it; they like it." Lavinia shouted in Vinnie's ear to make herself heard.

Then, looking across at Mr. Lincoln's white marble face, it seemed to Vinnie that he was weeping as often he had wept in life "while looking through the White House study window to the lawns where little Willie used to play." Quickly, Vinnie pulled herself together, for the tears being shed were her own.

Senator Lyman Trumbull of Illinois, a man who had always shown faith in Vinnie's capabilities, and Senator Matthew Carpenter from Vinnie's home state, Wisconsin, made complimentary speeches, praising both statue and sculptress. Senator Carpenter concluded with the following words:

Our artist was aware that no flattery was expected
at her hands. When the people employed her to
execute this work, they were in no mood for dis-
sembling. War is a severe teacher of sincerity and
truth. The people did not desire somebody's con-
ception of what a great leader of a mighty people,
in the most fearful crisis of their history, ought to
look like. But they did wish for an exact likeness of
Abraham Lincoln. And who was this Abraham Lincoln, the remembrance of whom they desired to
perpetuate? Was he like Jupiter or Apollo—like
Caesar or Cicero—like Cromwell or Napoleon? No,
no; like neither of these. And the people did not
employ Vinnie Ream to make a statue of either of
these, but of Abraham Lincoln as he appeared in the
White House, and there he appeared just as he did
on the prairies and in the court rooms of the West.

The great unveiling was over. It only remained for
General Sherman to lead Vinnie forward to receive the
cheering adulation of the crowd. This was her moment of
triumph! Even the cruel harassment to which she had been
subjected during the Johnson impeachment could now be
forgotten.

Back in the third tier the Senators from Kansas, Missouri, and Wisconsin were having a heated argument, for
each claimed Vinnie as his own state's native daughter.
Even when Matt Carpenter, the Senator from Wisconsin,
insisted that he remembered her as a babe near Madison
the others were unconvinced. Finally, Lavinia put an end
to their squabbling.

"My daughter," she firmly announced, "was born in
Wisconsin."

∽14∾

POEMS AND PROPOSALS

> Send toothache, plagues
>   or ghastly famine;
> Take wealth, take all the
>   hoards of mammon;
> Leave neither hope, nor fame,
>   nor riches,
> But save me from our modern
>   witches.

WITH A SMILE Vinnie tucked the poem into a large brown envelope pencil-marked VERSES. Since the unveiling of the Lincoln statue, every mail had contained such valentines. Two of the senders were well-known poets. In their own way, each was unusual.

Albert Pike, a bearded middle-aged gentleman with white hair flowing to his waist, had a grown-up daughter, Lillian, who was Vinnie's friend. Fame and financial remuneration for her sculpture had opened many doors to Vinnie, who was now accepted in some of Washington's most socially-prominent families.

On special occasions, such as New Year's Day, it was announced in the Washington newspapers that Lillian Pike and Vinnie would receive together. When General Pike developed an affection for Vinnie that was more than fatherly, she seems to have handled the delicate situation with good common sense. Deluged with the most passionate love poems, she somehow managed to evade the General's amorous advances while keeping his daughter's friendship. To the end of his days, Albert Pike never lost his affection for Vinnie Ream. In a handwritten poem "Cléopâtre," he declares:

> . . . be not so vain as to think
> That the sweet May can long love November

Though Vinnie was genuinely fond of him, she did not love him enough to become his wife.

The same applied to the poet, Cincinnatus Hiner Miller, who had renamed himself Joaquin to honor a Mexican bandit whose defense he had undertaken. Known to the ladies of Washington as "that dreadful Joaquin Miller," because of his several marriages, he, too, fell under Vinnie's spell. Although flattered, she bluntly told him she had no intention of being swept off on a horse, the way he had chosen to elope with one of his wives.

Lavinia was incensed when Joaquin came calling in chaps and sombrero, "which he wore indoors and out." Such small eccentricities did not worry Vinnie, for by this time she was used to the Bohemian manners of poets and artists. Besides, Joaquin's tales of his life with the Indians, among whom he had found his first wife, were always interesting. His half-Indian daughter had been given the beautiful name of Cali-Shasta.

When Vinnie refused his offer of marriage, Joaquin went off in search of literary fame. In all his letters he addressed her as "my dear, dear little Vinnie Ream."

During 1871, when she was friendly with Miller and Pike, her old acquaintance Boudy was in town. Now in his middle thirties and handsome as ever, he regularly asked Vinnie for her hand in marriage. Of all the friends she ever made, nobody occupied a closer spot in her heart than Boudy. Unfortunately, they had been friends too long, and he seemed to her like a brother.

"I am sorry to hear that you have accomplished little else but fame," he teased her in a letter. "You have got enough of that, conscience knows."

He searched out new songs "that I think you will like" for their frequent musical evenings, held at the fine new house she had bought off Pennsylvania Avenue. At all times he tried to obtain favorable sculpture commissions for her, but she could never decide whether she loved him enough for marriage. Besides, she was at the height of her fame, and marrying Boudy would have meant one day exchanging the cosmopolitan life of Washington for obscurity on a reservation. Elias Cornelius Boudinot paid his greatest tribute to Vinnie Ream by naming in her honor the town of Vinita, Oklahoma, which he founded upon Indian lands in 1871.

When Vinnie sang "The Coronach" for the first time in public at a concert, General William Tecumseh Sherman (who had marched through Georgia) escorted her to the piano. This was too much for Boudy, a former lieutenant colonel in the Confederate Army. He stormed out of the concert in disgust.

But Boudy was soon back again to sing "more sweet songs" at Vinnie's home. However, he was often jealous when he felt like it, as the following letter shows:

> When I was last in Terre Haute I caught a glimpse of a letter the superscription of which was in your handwriting. The letter was to a handsome young man. Where in the world did you get acquainted with him? You are not so much unlike other pretty young ladies as I used to think.
>
> Regards to your Mother,
> Ever yours,
> E.C.B.

Pleading the cause of his Indian people, while endeavoring to recover the property he had lost because of his Confederate leanings, Boudy made many friends as well as enemies in Washington. An honorable man, he was a credit to his race.

The names in Vinnie's charmed circle of friends read like a volume of *Who's Who*. They included General George Armstrong Custer, "half general and half scout," hero of Custer's Last Stand, which was to thrill future generations of American schoolboys.

Vinnie had good reason to remember General Custer. His aide had once disturbed her at four in the morning with the following urgent communication:

> My dear Vinnie,
> Pardon me for disturbing you at this early hour. Please have your servant examine the floor of your

studio to see if my wallet (not my pistol) was not dropped there last night.

As Vinnie had no servant available she was obliged to return to her studio in the icy hours of an early winter morning. She would gladly have "shot him" herself.

"Yellow-haired" General Custer, writing to her on February 13, 1871, movingly observed that "your victories are lasting and unlike mine are not purchased at the expense of the lifeblood of fellow creatures, leaving sorrow and desolation in their track."

Five years later, surrounded by three thousand of Chief Sitting Bull's Sioux warriors, Custer and his loyal detachment of two hundred and seventy-seven troopers were all to perish at the Little Bighorn.

In spite of the distractions of a wide circle of distinguished friends and admirers, Vinnie's fame in the field of sculpture continued to grow. Contrary to the opinions of those who had predicted that she could hardly hope to obtain commissions which would equal that of the Lincoln statue, Vinnie's work was much in demand. She was paid the sum of fifteen hundred dollars to make a marble bust of Lincoln for Cornell University. A similar fee was paid her for a bust of Mayor Samuel S. Powell of Brooklyn, which was to stand over the Speaker's Desk in the City Council Room. In 1874, another Mayor of Brooklyn, John W. Hunter, appointed her official sculptor of the town. The *Graphic*, in its issue of March 30, 1875, called Vinnie Ream "the Charlotte Brontë of Sculpture."

Other honors came her way. A distinctive model of

the Indian girl Anna Guy, whom Vinnie's brother Bob had married, was cast in bronze and bought by the Mayor of St. Louis.

For their scrapbooks, admirers solicited photographs of her figure of Miriam, the sister of Moses, leading the women of Israel in a song of thanksgiving after they had safely crossed the Red Sea. A Philadelphia woman paid three thousand dollars for a life-size copy of this work in marble—a sizable sum in those days. Critics noted the graceful posture of Vinnie's Miriam, "dancing draperies blown back . . . holding a timbrel over her head."

Vinnie also made a series of figures representing the land of America, the West being portrayed by a "hardy young girl, draperies blown by prairie winds."

Ironically enough, Vinnie Ream's native Wisconsin still had not assigned her the commission she most desired. In 1868 a state senate resolution (adopted by a two-thirds vote in the Wisconsin Legislature, but later lost in the Assembly) had, according to the Hoxie family papers in the Library of Congress refused "to award to her a contract for supplying pieces of sculpture to fill the empty niches assigned to the State of Wisconsin in the National Capitol at Washington."

As if to pour oil upon troubled waters, for her pride was hurt, the Legislature's Executive resolved "That the refusal of this Legislature to award to her [Vinnie Ream] a contract for said statues at this time is by no means based upon a want of appreciation of her worth as a lady, or her genius as a sculptor, but rather upon the inability of the

State to incur at present the pecuniary obligations conse-
quent on such contract."

As Boudy told her when she heard the disappointing
news, "A prophet is without honor in his own country."
His words made her think of Georg Brandes who had
known a similar experience in his native Denmark. Fondly,
she recalled a letter received from George Healy, the
painter, in which he said:

> Of all those nice people I met at your house [in
> Rome] the only one who called in time to see your
> picture was the young Dane.

However, Vinnie had small cause for complaint when
she paused to consider her phenomenal rise to fame and
prosperity. The Abbeville *Medium*, in its issue of February
19, 1873, sums it all up very well:

> Miss Vinnie is an admirable specimen of our insti-
> tutions. She lives now in a nice house, owned by
> herself, on the Avenue between Second and Third,
> and almost under the shadow of the massive dome
> of the capitol; and in her study is seen a picture of a
> log cabin with slab roof and located in the wilds of
> Wisconsin, her birth place, and near it a beautiful
> young girl wreathed with flowers. You are struck
> with its loveliness and you gaze at it and turn
> around and look at the artist and you see at once
> the likeness. She . . . has been so successful in rais-
> ing herself from obscurity to eminence.

✑15✑

THE MOST BEAUTIFUL GIRL
IN BROOKLYN

I⊤ ᴡᴀꜱ a beautiful day in early June of 1876. Vinnie was visiting her sister and brother-in-law, Major and Mrs. Perry Fuller in New York. They were trying to persuade her to open a studio in the city. However, Vinnie was not sure that such a move would be wise. Away from home only a month, she already missed Washington.

That afternoon Mary Fuller had an engagement which afforded Vinnie the opportunity she had been awaiting to visit the Green Wood Cemetery in Brooklyn. This might appear a strange place for a young woman to go, but not a young woman who was a sculptress. The Green Wood Cemetery was famed for its outstanding statuary and monuments which were set on a hillside that had been landscaped with weeping mulberries and willow trees, giant tree hydrangeas, and rare copper beeches. It conveyed the impression of being a lovely park rather than a resting place of the dead.

Vinnie dismissed her hired carriage at the entrance gates, preferring to explore on foot. Walking up what appeared to be a main thoroughfare, wide enough for two carriages to pass with ease, she stopped suddenly, thinking that her ears deceived her. Somebody was playing a guitar!

Curious, she turned up a narrow lane past a signpost reading "Verdant Path." Turning the corner, she found the source of the mysterious melody, for sitting in her carriage and attended by an elderly coachman, was a middle-aged woman "with large gray eyes . . . her face showing traces of once having known an exquisite beauty." Softly plucking the strings of her guitar, she seemed quite oblivious to the world around her.

Vinnie, embarrassed at invading her privacy, tried to escape unseen by tiptoeing up a grassy bank. She had only gone a short distance when, with a cry of surprise, she tripped over a girl who was sitting under a lilac bush reading a book of poetry, her rich reddish-brown hair falling, like Vinnie's, to her shoulders. She was dressed in a close-fitting gown of the palest green taffeta with wide frilly cuffs. Vinnie, hastening to apologize, was already appraising the strange girl's potential as a model.

"Her neck," wrote Vinnie later, "was long like a swan . . . her skin white and unblemished." Vinnie had only once seen so perfect a complexion, and that was her mother's. Lavinia had taken pride in reminding her husband that the girls in her family were often called "the white McDonalds," because of their fair skin.

The beautiful young woman graciously accepted Vinnie's apologies, saying that in any case she should not have been idly sitting there while her aunt was "planting geraniums on Willy's grave." Vinnie understandably looked surprised, for if the lady in the carriage was the aunt, she certainly was not planting geraniums.

The stranger seemed to follow Vinnie's train of thought, for she began to smile. "I have two aunts," she explained. "Aunt Lydia you probably saw sitting in our carriage. Aunt Sarah is further up on the mound." She waved her hand in the direction of a tall obelisk. Sure enough, there was a small dark-clad figure who was certainly planting something.

"Come, I will introduce you to my aunts," volunteered the young woman; "although, like me, I feel they will remember you. Are you not Miss Vinnie Ream, the sculptress?"

Vinnie stammered that this was correct, at the same time assisting the stranger to her feet.

"We were among the crowd the day Mayor Hunter appointed you Brooklyn's official sculptor. How proud we were that such an honor had at long last come to one of our own sex. My aunts are both staunch fighters in the battle to improve feminine rights."

Vinnie expressed her thanks, wondering at the same time if she were about to meet two formidable "Lizzie Stantons."

The young woman told Vinnie that her name was Martha Hasseltine Cummings, and that she was an orphan who had been brought up by her aunts. Upon reaching the obelisk she introduced Vinnie to Sarah Marion Combes, who was much plainer than the woman in the carriage. Vinnie guessed that even in the flower of youth Mrs. Combes had never been considered beautiful. Then she read the inscription upon the obelisk's base.

William C. Combes
Son of Hiram G. Combes and Sarah M. Combes
Born Nov. 14, 1848
Died Nov. 4, 1874

Martha's Aunt Sarah followed Vinnie's eyes. "He was my only son," she explained. "Martha and he were brought up together. They were like brother and sister."

"We find it hard to believe that he has gone," Martha said. "Twenty-six is young to die."

"He was training to be a doctor," explained Mrs. Combes. "So many of our young men were lost in the war. Those, like Willy, who were left needed to interest themselves in useful occupations."

"My brother served with the Confederate cavalry," Vinnie told them.

"I lost two brothers at Gettysburg," said Sarah, adding as an afterthought, "on the Union side."

Vinnie looked down at the red geraniums Mrs. Combes had planted. Against the gray granite their petals made her think of drops of blood.

"Come," said Mrs. Combes, "you must meet Mrs. Harris, Martha's other aunt, for in a way you have much in common. She paints."

"And so do you," said Martha, slipping her hand through her aunt's arm as they descended the steep slope.

"Porcelain plates for church bazaars," replied Aunt Sarah rather tartly. It was the first time that Vinnie had seen her smile. "My sister is a real artist."

Lydia Wooster Harris was still happily playing her

guitar when the others reached her. She was accompanying herself as she sang "The Battle Hymn of the Republic," which Julia Ward Howe, another feminist, had written. "Sister, how militant you sound!" Mrs. Combes finally made herself heard.

"Aunty Lyd," as Martha affectionately called her musical aunt, was not in the least embarrassed. "I enjoy playing my guitar," she explained with warmth in her voice. "I learned to play it when I was three. It is my firm belief that all baby girls should do the same."

"I know," said Martha.

"This is Miss Vinnie Ream, the sculptress of President Lincoln." Mrs. Combes seemed quite excited. "You remember, Lydia; she modeled Peter Cooper from life. . . ."

"Of course," snapped Mrs. Harris; then, looking in Vinnie's direction, she said, "Perhaps Miss Ream will honor us by taking a cup of hot chocolate."

Vinnie had really come to see the marble statues on the monuments, yet she hadn't the heart to say no. Besides, Mrs. Harris interested her very much. "If I *have* to grow old, please God may I remain pretty as she," Vinnie wrote after the meeting.

A few minutes later all four ladies were being driven to Number 224 Carroll Street, Brooklyn.

Over the chocolate cups they all became better acquainted. "I shall be Mrs. Whitney in just ten days," exclaimed Martha, her beautiful eyes sparkling happily. "Mrs. Joseph Botsford Whitney."

Mrs. Harris snorted, "Even when Lucy Stone the

great reformer saw fit to take a husband, she *never* changed her name."

"Oh, Aunty Lyd!" Martha pouted. "You did not remain Miss Cummings when you married Uncle Edward. You became Mrs. Harris."

Mrs. Harris took a large sip of hot chocolate and immediately changed the subject, for the mention of the ill-fated Mr. Harris was particularly distasteful to her. It was also something of an embarrassment to Mrs. Combes, for her sister had married on the rebound, as it were.

Lydia Harris had been very much in love with Hiram Combes, a promising young executive for Wanamaker's, the fashionable New York store. Unfortunately, Sarah Combes, who was much plainer looking than her sister, had loved him too.

For two whole days poor Sarah had cried and cried until, in sheer desperation, Lydia shouted, "If you want him so much, you may have him."

Sarah took her at her word. Mr. Combes never had a say in the matter!

A few months later Lydia met and married an Englishman, Edward Harris. With him, she sailed for England, where she painted a portrait of the poet Algernon Charles Swinburne's sister Isabella, bought a brass tea urn, and then returned to America. Poor Mr. Harris was left alone in England, while Aunty Lyd spent the rest of her life fighting for women's rights. All this Martha told Vinnie in the privacy of her bedroom where they had retired to chat.

She also told Vinnie how she had met Joseph Whitney, a most interesting young silk merchant who, as a boy, had been on the first ship into Japan after Commodore Perry had landed there.

"He walked about with his own guard," said Martha with pride.

Then she showed Vinnie the Satsuma porcelain Mr. Whitney had bought in the Orient. Vinnie examined the exquisite workmanship. In each small vase or pot was a scroll on which Joseph had written his interpretation of the figures painted on the exterior.

Vinnie liked Martha, in spite of the fact that she did not usually enjoy the company of women. She even envied Martha a little, as she talked happily about Joseph Whitney who was only the second man in her life.

"The other one was Aunty Lyd's choice. She will never forgive me for refusing him, but he was much too old. He had long whiskers and came from Chicago," Martha whispered in Vinnie's ear. "He was a millionaire, and he drank. Look." She pointed to a metal sculpture of two warring sparrows. "His farewell gift! Most appropriate, don't you agree? After all, we were always quarreling."

Vinnie nodded her head. She wanted to tell Martha about Boudy and Georg Brandes and some of her own conquests. But first there was the successful Mr. Whitney to hear about.

"We met on a horse-drawn streetcar," confessed Martha. "He had been mending his father's greenhouse and he ran out of nails. Now, wasn't that fate, for on the way to buy more it was my streetcar upon which he alighted. . . . Although he was wearing his working suit and Aunty Lyd says no real gentleman ever addresses a lady in his working suit—before I had reached the end of my journey, he proposed and I accepted!"

Vinnie admitted that she had received many proposals, but never one quite so romantic. "Except perhaps on a certain ride with a dashing young Dane in the purple dusk of the Roman *campagna*."

She did not have time to explain why she did not accept his offer, for at that moment Mrs. Combes knocked on the door.

"It is the minister," she said to Martha, smiling apologetically at Vinnie. "I do not think you should keep him waiting."

"The Reverend Henry Ward Beecher," explained Martha to Vinnie. "He is a friend of the family."

"But not such a friend that he must ruin the best parlor table with his blessed collection of stones."

"Stones?" Vinnie looked inquiringly at Mrs. Combes.

Everybody knew that Harriet Beecher Stowe's brother was one of the most eloquent preachers of his day and an outspoken champion of women's suffrage—but stones, blessed or otherwise—what did that mean?

It was Martha who did the explaining as she and Vinnie, with arms interlinked, went down the twisting, red mahogany staircase to the front door. For a hobby, the Reverend Beecher collected small uncut semi-precious stones. He kept them in a cloth bag in his pocket, just as small boys carried marbles. Whatever the occasion, when he came calling upon Aunt Lydia and Aunt Sarah, out came his little bag, the contents of which he enjoyed spreading on the top of their highly polished table.

Vinnie would have liked meeting Henry Ward Beecher, but now the carriage was ready to take her to the ferry on which she would go to Manhattan.

∾16∾

MARRIED AT LAST

THIRTY-ONE YEARS old and still the toast of Washington—as one masculine admirer noted, "Presidents go but Vinnie goes on forever." In an era when women married young, she seemed to be the exception. Among her birthday greetings in 1878 had been a letter from Martha Hasseltine Cummings, now Mrs. Joseph Botsford Whitney. Vinnie read it somewhat enviously, for Martha, although not yet twenty-three, had already been married two years.

Being one of the capital's most eligible spinsters, mention of Vinnie regularly appeared in the society gossip columns. Into a blue-and-gold scrapbook she pasted the more favorable of these mentions, including the following amusing tidbit:

> Vinnie Ream and a noted singer were recently at a reception together, and it is stated with surprise by a fashion paper, that Vinnie received the more attention of the two. This seems but right however. It is impossible that a solitary singer should compare with the pretty chiseler of marble, when it ordinarily takes twenty choirs to make a Ream.

It is understandable that Vinnie should be receiving so much attention, for she had already embarked upon the second most important sculpture of her career, the statue

of Admiral David Glasgow Farragut, famed for his block-
ade of the Bay of Mobile. To the Americans of his generation, Farragut occupied a place comparable to that
which Nelson held for the British.

Born at Stony Point, near Knoxville, Tennessee, July
5, 1801, Farragut entered the Navy as a midshipman at the
age of nine. Serving aboard the frigate *Essex*, he was
wounded in its first engagement with the enemy. In his
report of the battle, Admiral David Dixon Porter gave
young David honorable mention, adding regretfully that
he was "too young for promotion."

Farragut's brilliant exploits in the Federal Navy during the Civil War made him a favorite of orators and poets.
The poet and physician, Oliver Wendell Holmes, wrote of
this national hero:

> I give the name that fits him best,
> Ay, better than his own—
> The Sea-king of the Sovereign West
> Who made his mast a throne!

Following the Civil War, Farragut was given charge
of the European Command. Here, he was enthusiastically
received with honor, personally inspecting the ironclad
fleets of England, Russia, and France. In 1866, Congress
made him a vice-admiral. Two years later, he was made
admiral, a rank which, prior to that time, had not existed
in the United States Navy. When, on August 14, 1870, he
died at Portsmouth, New Hampshire, there was national
mourning.

By a joint resolution approved April 16, 1872, Congress instructed special committees of the Senate and House to inspect models for a colossal statue of the late Admiral. Among the notable sculptors submitting plans were Clark Mills and his former pupil, Vinnie Ream.

The committees of the House and Senate could not agree, so they were replaced by a commission consisting of the Admiral's widow, General William Tecumseh Sherman, and Secretary of the Navy George Maxwell Robeson. When the commission officially met at the Arlington Hotel in Washington on November 20, 1872, estimates of cost were agreed upon, after which the coveted contract (which, apart from its prestige value, would result in a payment of twenty thousand dollars for the successful sculptor) was awarded to Vinnie Ream.

Vinnie's good fortune raised a cry of protest from relatives and friends of the unsuccessful competitors, especially since it was common knowledge that General Sherman thought very highly of her. He was, however, not Vinnie's only champion, for Mrs. Farragut had also taken a notion to befriend her. When Vinnie complained bitterly of the injustice of some of the unfavorable comments being hurled at her by the popular press, Mrs. Farragut advised, "Don't be the least discouraged by adverse criticism, for it is impossible for anyone to achieve greatness in any way without being a target to be shot at from the quiver of envy."

Vinnie responded by repeating to Mrs. Farragut what Clark Mills had once told her, "Clay is a pliable and wonderful material, and readily responds to the loving touch of genius."

Vinnie pledged herself "to the Secretary of the Navy, General of the Army, and through Mrs. Farragut to the whole Nation to do my best." She then signed the contract "with a steady hand and air of destiny."

Her new assignment presented problems to Vinnie, for in order to house her proposed model she had to remove the floor-boards and cut a hole in the ceiling of her studio. Perched like a small bird on a high stool, her hair hidden by a turban, she slowly molded the gigantic figure of the hero-Admiral. Mrs. Farragut was a frequent visitor to the studio for, apart from the statue, she had special plans for her protégée.

A matrimonial matchmaker, she had already picked a husband for Vinnie. The best friend of her son, Loyall Farragut, the man she had chosen was Lieutenant Richard Leveridge Hoxie of the United States Engineers, a promising young career soldier who, with Lieutenant W. L. Marchael, had in 1875 published for the Military Service Institute a pamphlet lengthily entitled "Instructions for Taking and Recording Meteorological Observations and for Preserving and Repairing the Instruments . . ."

Tall, fair, and handsome, Lieutenant Hoxie was admirably aided and abetted in his pursuit of Vinnie by the indomitable Mrs. Farragut, who brought them together upon every possible occasion. Discovering from Lavinia that Vinnie was particularly partial to mountain laurel (as

Lavinia also was), Vinnie's studio soon took on the appearance of a hillside in the Adirondacks. Of all the men Vinnie had ever known, Richard Hoxie was the most persistent. Whenever she sent him away so that she could proceed in peace with her work, he was always back with more mountain laurel in the morning.

When her plaster cast was found mysteriously smashed, it was Richard now and not Boudy who comforted her. Starting once more with the double encouragement of Richard and the Matchmaker, Vinnie's progress was not again impeded. Richard continued to propose marriage until one day in a fit of temperament Vinnie exploded, "Wait until my statue is finished."

Richard was willing, but not Mrs. Farragut, who persuaded Vinnie that for once love should have its way. Somewhat reluctantly, Vinnie agreed to complete her model after the honeymoon.

All Washington was agog with the news of the wedding planned for May 28th. Boudy refused point-blank to attend. Albert Pike, Vinnie's patriarchal admirer, sat down to write what would be her last token of love from his pen. It was entitled, "Must we say Goodbye, Darling, Must we say Goodbye."

Mary Fuller, Vinnie's sister, arrived in Washington to help Lavinia with preparations for the lavish wedding, which for brilliance was rivaled only by that of Nellie Grant, the former President's daughter.

As the great day approached, Vinnie dismayed her

mother by refusing to carry the traditional bridal bouquet. Lavinia said that she could at least carry a spray of mountain laurel, but her suggestion went unheeded, for Richard had bought Vinnie enough branches to last her a lifetime. *"I shall carry a fan."* She was adamant.

Lavinia was shocked and Mary, now a great lady in New York society, was outraged. To add insult to injury, Vinnie also refused the conventional orange-blossom wreath, preferring instead a white turban with a billowing veil hanging from the back. The bridal gown showed off to perfection her small, plumpish figure—and she did condescend to have a train.

On the morning of the wedding, Richard found the newspapers full of doleful poems from Vinnie's various rejected beaus.

Wrote Albert Pike:

> Must we say "Goodbye!"
> Darling?
> Ah! word so hard to say!
> Must we, so long adoring
> Give you to him, today?

Richard swallowed hard. Being very proud of his Lieutenant's rank, he didn't particularly care to be called "him" in a daily column.

If Albert was hurt that Vinnie should be getting married, his daughter Lillian was not. She seized the opportunity to write Vinnie for "a piece of carpet large enough to cover a good size footstool . . . You will save me some ex-

pense and oblige me very much." Doubtless she thought
that Vinnie might have some leftovers from furnishing
her new home.

When Vinnie (with her fan) entered the fashionable
Church of the Ascension to the strains of a bridal quartet
written for male voices by the rejected Albert Pike,
Richard, resplendent in military uniform, was waiting at
the chancel steps to receive her. As Robert Ream was ill,
General Sherman gave the bride away. The service, attended by everyone of note in Washington, and others—
such as Martha Whitney—from further afield, was per-
formed by Bishop William Pinckney, a friend of Vinnie's,
assisted by the Reverend John H. Elliott, minister of the
church.

> For, at Hymen's alter stands
> To be wed
> A crown'd head.

Thus did Mrs. A. L. Ruter Dufour describe Vinnie
Ream on her wedding day.

≈17≈

THE FARRAGUT

THE FIRST thing that Richard Hoxie did after breakfast on the first day of his honeymoon was to make his wife promise never again to supply a department-store testimonial. More than once in the past she had shocked Washington society by granting such favors, in an era when a lady's name was supposed only to appear in the newspaper at the time of her marriage and her death.

Born to wealth, Richard was determined from the beginning that no wife of his was going to work for pay. Perhaps because she had been a breadwinner for so long, Vinnie agreed. After "the Farragut," as they familiarly referred to the current project, was completed she would give her services only to charitable causes. This, Richard assured her, was the only recipe for a "perfect marriage."

On June 4th, Mary wrote that "she [Lavinia] took so much satisfaction in putting up the [wedding cake] and sending it about." Mary asked at the same time if Vinnie would not like her wedding finery sent to West Point, where the couple was spending part of their honeymoon. She had read "there is to be a grand hop on the 12th instant."

Elizabeth B. Custer, General Custer's widow, was delighted that Vinnie had in the end married a soldier. Writing upon black-edged notepaper she said:

> I was so afraid last winter that you would let the hours of your life slip by without entering that charmed state which is the rounding to every woman's life.

When she requested Vinnie to make a bust of the ill-fated General Custer, Richard insisted that Vinnie could undertake the commission only as a gift. He had, however, reckoned without Mrs. Custer's pride, which led her to stubbornly insist upon making payment.

"My dear Mrs. Hoxie," she addressed the young matron:

> I don't know what sentence to frame that may prove how excellent I think the likeness of General Custer is, as I saw it in the clay . . .

She goes on to say:

> I am so glad in these days of false ideas of that most sacred of ties—*marriage,* Mr. Hoxie and yourself had the courage to make a real love match.

Mrs. Custer seems to have been pressed for money, as in another communication she reveals:

> I have almost saved enough to send you the check for the amount. In a short time I will send you a check for one hundred dollars. . . . I am so proud of it for I have earned it myself.

Mrs. Bingham, the understanding widow of George Caleb Bingham, wrote on December 12, 1879, requesting that Vinnie let her have the bust she had made of the painter, who had died five months before.

Back in Washington, the new Mrs. Hoxie worked hard to complete "the Farragut," delivering her completed model to the Washington Navy Yard in 1880, where, under the direction of competent engineers, it was to be reproduced in bronze. At Vinnie's suggestion the metal used came from the Propeller of Admiral Farragut's flagship, the USS *Hartford*, in which he had so often tasted victory.

Nine months were to elapse before the statue's casting was completed, during which time Vinnie made many trips of inspection to the Navy Yard. The Dahlgren Ordnance Building had become a giant studio, which intrigued not only important Army, Navy, and civil visitors but flocks of seagulls as well. The gulls would sweep through the building's open doors to settle happily on Admiral Farragut's head. The model stood on an elevated platform, eighteen feet high, with a revolving stone underneath. Another platform, suspended from the roof beams by a block and tackle was built around the figure and could be drawn up and down as the work required. Over everything hung the acrid smell of the roaring foundry fires.

This was a time of anxiety, not only for Vinnie but for the engineers over the first attempt ever made at metal casting in the Navy Yard. Theirs was a combined triumph, when each separate piece of bronze emerged flawless from the enormous molds. The original clay model had taken Vinnie three years to prepare. Six molds were required: the head and shoulders formed one section; then each arm was cast separately, while the lower part of the body and plinth went together; the sword and marine glass were each cast in an original mold.

The dedication and unveiling was an important event in the life of the capital. April 25, 1881, was chosen, and all of Washington took a holiday in the spring sunshine. Business closed down for the afternoon; schoolrooms were emptied, and even Congress adjourned. Bunting and streamers hung from public and private buildings; flags waved jauntily in the breeze.

A contingent of marines and sailors, marching in formation, escorted the President's carriage. They had arrived by rail from the ships of the North Atlantic squadron, which was anchored off Alexandria. Never before, it was said, had so large a Naval group been seen together at one time in the streets of Washington.

Proudly riding in the same carriage as President and Mrs. James Abram Garfield were Mrs. Farragut and Mrs. Richard Hoxie. Less than three months later, when the President met his untimely death at the hands of an assassin, Vinnie was to recall his kind words of praise at the Farragut unveiling.

In spite of the crowds, it was remembered by an eyewitness that there was no dust. The procession wound its way from the Naval Monument at the Western entrance of the Capitol grounds along Pennsylvania Avenue to Fifteenth Street, terminating at the newly named Farragut Square. Occupying the place of honor in the square's center was the colossal bronze figure draped in the national colors. At each corner of the pedestal were banked exotic potted plants in full bloom, contributed by the botanical gardens. Three special platforms had been erected for the most important visitors. Mrs. Farragut and Vinnie shared the same one as the President and his lady. Beyond them, for many blocks, stretched a rippling sea of human faces.

As the President was seated, another procession came into view, led by two hundred members of the Grand Army of the Republic, carrying white silk guidons embroidered with the badges of their own Army corps. After them marched the Army in all its glory, including "noble gray-haired heroes of Mexico." Bands played, the crowds cheered lustily, and children waved little paper flags sold for a penny apiece.

At last the great moment of actual unveiling arrived, as later described in graphic detail by the Washington *Evening Star*:

> The statue was then unveiled. This part of the programme fell to the hands of the Quartermaster Knowles, who was with the Admiral on the flagship when he was lashed to the rigging at the battle of Mobile Bay. He was assisted by James Wiley, who was boatswain on the same flagship. During the ceremony of unveiling, Bartholomew Diggins hoisted and hauled down the Admiral's flag. The unveiling was of itself full of incidents; an admiral's flag was displayed; the drums of the several bands beat four ruffles; the Marine band played an appropriate selection, while in the rear at Lafayette square an admiral's salute of 16 guns was fired from a naval battery. At the sound of the first gun the troops came

to a "carry" arms, and when the last was fired, to a "parade rest."

A great shout went up from the multitude as the flag that veiled the statue was withdrawn, showing the figure and features of the grand old naval captain. He is represented standing on the deck of his famous flagship, the Hartford, with one foot resting on a pulley-block, and with a telescopic glass in his hand. The face and pose of the old hero combine at once to tell the story of his character, and that of the great task before him, and which for the time being commands his soul and all his faculties. The expression is thoroughly characteristic, resolute, watchful, reliant. The figure is ten feet in height, and, at its elevation, is a most noble and impressive one.

On May 5, 1881, Vinnie read with much satisfaction what Mary Clemmer Ames, the famed woman newspaper correspondent, had to say of her new masterpiece:

It has its own significance, the fact that this statue of an American hero, which is to go down to posterity, was chosen by a woman and wrought by a woman. When, ten years ago, it was decided by Congress that a statue should be erected to keep living and present before coming generations the presence and person of the great Admiral, many masters in art sent their models from different parts of the world, each hoping to be the chosen competitor. After prolonged deliberation and discussion the committee of selection accepted the model preferred and chosen by Mrs. Farragut—a full-length portrait untouched by allegory; just the man himself, the Admiral leaning slightly forward, yet with head erect, with face attent, glass in hand, as he had stood many hundred times, gazing out over distant seas. Just a man on watch, a man on duty, with the true heart of a patriot in his breast, the unflinching eyes of a sailor in his head, and the undaunted front of a hero ready to die, if need be, for his country.

For the completed statue, including pedestal and placing, the sculptor received from the United States government the sum of $25,000. Washington is a city of statues as well as of magnificent distances, but this was the first monument erected to the memory of a naval officer. It not only commemorates the heroism of a great sea-captain, but also the courage and perseverance of an American woman, who, in this, her greatest work of art, has embodied the highest expression of her genius.

❧ 18 ❧

THE PERFECT MARRIAGE

Richard built his bride a home overlooking "the Farragut," which they would occupy when his military duties did not require his presence elsewhere.

1883 was a happy year for Vinnie. When her son was born, she called him Richard, after his father—Richie for short. He had "fluffy fair hair." His father bought him a rocking horse. On most days Vinnie could be seen sitting at the window of her Washington home with the baby on her knee. Somewhat wistfully, she would look out upon "the Farragut," which she then believed was her last work.

Writing from Chicago, Mrs. George Peter Alexander Healy, wife of the artist who had painted Vinnie in Rome, said, "We should be glad to see photographs of your handsome husband and child."

With proper grandmotherly fatuousness, Lavinia begged in one of her letters, "Dear little Richie, talk kindly of me to him."

Upon his wife and his son, Richard, senior—who described himself as "a proud old-fashioned husband"—lavished all the luxury at his command.

As Vinnie had a young child, her sister Mary made the arrangements for the celebration of their parents' golden wedding, which was held in Washington on Saturday, October 31, 1885. Robert Ream was too ill to come downstairs, so that the Reverend Dr. Sunderland resolemnized the marriage at his bedside. On November 21st of that same year, Mr. Ream was dead, and Vinnie pasted a poem by Elizabeth Barrett Browning into her scrapbook:

> All are not taken; there are left behind
> Living beloveds, tender looks to bring
> And make the daylight still a happy thing,
> And tender voices to make soft the wind.

She was doubtless thinking of Richie.

Offering a bust of her father to the State Historical Society of Wisconsin, she was told by letter that such a gift would be "a noble addition to our rapidly growing gallery." Vinnie had loved her father, seeing him always as the curly brown-haired pioneer, standing in sun and wind, surveying the distant prairie lands.

On April 16th of that same year Vinnie had received a very different kind of shock, when Boudy—"her Boudy" —then forty-nine years old, married Clara C. Minear, twenty-five, of San Francisco, in Washington's First Presbyterian Church. Still wearing his cowboy hat and hair grown well below his shoulders, Boudy immediately left the city with his wife to resume his law practice in Fort Smith, Arkansas.

Vinnie's womanly vanity was somewhat appeased when a few months later he saw fit to write her:

> As I was walking down from our pretty little house
> this morning to my office, my thoughts drifted to

you, the porch was covered with vines and ablaze with morning glories . . .

Was this the same porch where he had first courted Vinnie so many years before? Boudy ended his letter by mentioning "our good friend" General Van Valkenburg, who had recently died:

> He always kept it in his parlor—the bust you made of me, twenty years—just think of it, twenty years ago.

Boudy's marriage was short-lived, for on September 27, 1890, he also died. The last words that he said were "Vinnie Ream."

> I feel great gratitude that my loving self-sacrificing Parents lived to see me comfortable and doing well. To see me under the care and protection of a man whom they loved and respected, and to see my bright little child honoring them.

This, Vinnie had written at the time of her mother's death, April 17, 1893.

By using the term "self-sacrificing," she exonerated her parents from the charge of Washington gossips that due to Robert's careless handling of her money, Vinnie had been near bankruptcy at the time of her marriage to Richard Hoxie. Both Robert and Lavinia Ream were hurt by the implications made in their lifetime that they "had sponged on Vinnie." Mary, their other daughter, in her own words "humored" Lavinia's "whims and fancies" during her last days. She felt obliged to mention the cackling tongues in a short handwritten family history she compiled on the Ream family.

Mary's unhappiness following the death of her husband, Major Fuller, was at times a shadow on Vinnie's own happiness.

"Indeed who has much sunshine after youth has gone?" bemoans Mary in one of her long, sad letters to her sister. "I can never tell you how lonely I am and I may live for years and years."

This was written in 1895, and she was still very much alive when Vinnie died.

Perry Fuller, a wealthy man with three splendid homes —in Lawrence, Kansas; New York City; and Washington (the two last had cost twenty-two thousand dollars and twenty-five thousand dollars respectively, large sums for those days)—already had four children when he married Mary. She bore him two of her own. The family lived lavishly, with many servants to wait upon them. Fuller is said to have driven the finest team of horses in New York's Central Park. His wealth seems suddenly to have vanished, for at his death Mary found herself penniless, and had to go into government service again. This, after having known so much luxury, she did with ill grace.

Vinnie's home life was happy with her two Richards, although there were times when she yearned to return to her art. The little family moved at intervals, wherever Richard, senior's, work should call them. Always what was described in *La Follette's Magazine* as Vinnie's "magnetism and very discriminating intelligence" drew callers from all parts of the world to meet the woman sculptor who, at the height of her success, "gave up her career for love."

Young Richie was a great favorite with the guests. There are two interesting contemporary photographs showing him with his mother. In one, as a child of four or five with closely-cropped fair hair, wearing a large floppy bow tie and high button-up boots, he sits quietly reading at his mother's feet. Vinnie, grown pleasantly plump, is seen playing a harp, the top of which is decorated with carved angels. On either side are some of her statues.

In the other picture, Richie, wearing a sailor suit and several years older, has a dove in his hand and another perched upon his shoulder. When she saw the finished photograph, Vinnie thought nostalgically of Georg Brandes and of those doves which he held while crossing the Roman *campagna*. She decided to break her silence of so many years to send him Richie's picture and her own. Writing from Copenhagen on February 20, 1907, Georg replied:

> It was a great joyful surprise for me to receive your letter and know, that you had not been malcontent with the manner in which you stood in my memory. Alas! how many years are gone! I feel yet as then, you too I believe, but a whole life separates us as we are now from where we were.
>
> My life as a writer has been a life of struggle,

victorious at last . . . I was married in 1876 and have
one daughter who married this January and is well.

> I am of all my heart
> truly and affectionate
> Yours,
> Georg Brandes

Vinnie, with her usual feminine vanity, carefully preserved this letter, together with the photograph he had sent.
He had grown stouter with the years, but, she noticed with
satisfaction, he had not lost his "good head of hair" through
which he "so dearly loved to run his fingers."

The "dreadful" poet Joaquin Miller had not forgotten her either. In 1893, he saw fit to address her once
more by letter as "My dear, dear little Vinnie Ream." He
told her that Robert Roosevelt, the political reformer and
conservationist, who at his suggestion had visited the Hoxies, had declared, "The world owes her [Vinnie Ream] a
debt for being so delightful." This same Robert Roosevelt
was the uncle of future president Theodore Roosevelt.

Visiting the Hoxies in 1897 at Portland, Maine, where
they were living next to the house in which the poet Long-
fellow was born, a Mrs. Isadore Baker writing in *The
Midland Monthly* of November, 1897, found the woman
once called the "Daughter of the Capitol" still "full of
Energy" and "just as determined . . . She is a ready talker,
never at a loss for a word, a simile, a sentence or an inci-
dent." Her home was filled with books, pictures and curios,
"each with a story."

Vinnie had not been very strong since Richie's birth,
having suffered from a chronic kidney ailment since that

time. This was the reason there had been no other children. After a particularly tiresome bout with illness she had confessed to Richard just how much she "missed her work." Being in charge of pottery stands at expositions was all very well, but she longed *really* to work again. Secretly, she was afraid her hands might have lost their once magic touch.

Richard, who still saw himself as her "protector," finally gave in to her pleading when a close family friend, the widow of Iowa's Civil War Governor Samuel Jordan Kirkwood, begged Vinnie to execute his statue in bronze. The problem remained—was she now strong enough for the stupendous task?

Having given Vinnie permission to work again, Richard, with his methodical engineering mind, began to think of ways of easing any physical strain for her. In a letter dated August 12, 1906, he begins:

> At Home
>
> I have been all day planning devices for enabling you to work at the statue and have not yet decided upon the best one. You will not be able to stand up as you did with the Farragut; but must work from a chair and this ought to be easily lifted and lowered, by yourself, if necessary. Perhaps the best arrangements will be a "boatswain's chair" with a differential pulley block for lifting and lowering. Neither can you climb ladders as you did, and I think they should be eliminated.

Obviously, Richard's invention helped, for after eighteen years of inactivity when Vinnie took up sculpture again the critics noted a "marked improvement in her work." The statue of Governor Kirkwood, when completed, was presented by the State of Iowa to National Statuary Hall, and Vinnie's bust of him was presented to Iowa University. The statue was cast by the Roman Bronze Works in Brooklyn, New York, and unveiled November 5, 1927.

A curious note creeps into that same letter written "At Home" by Richard and signed: "Goodnight—I love you, Papa." It concerns Richie, or Richard as his father called him.

> I hope Richard has settled down to honest work—four hours daily—and is learning to make himself useful and agreeable. He can never work outside until he does so . . .

What was wrong with Richie, Vinnie's "bright little son?" Why does his father appear to have lost patience with him?

Information concerning Richie, Vinnie's only child, is vague and sketchy. We do know that he entered an osteopathic institution in Missouri, where later he died. The nature of his bone or muscular disease is unknown. He was still living at the time of his mother's death, although Richard, in the posthumous memoirs he compiled of his wife, makes no direct mention of their son. The boy's name slips briefly into a lone newspaper obituary.

There is a photograph of Richie owned by Mary Paxton Keeley—who has studied Vinnie Ream for many years—which she describes as ". . . taken when he was between two and three on a rocking horse. The photographer was Alex Gardner, Washington. He [Richie] looks bright enough in that. Perhaps some accident did something to him later."

Wistfully, the little boy in the sailor suit fades into obscurity.

Richard retired August 7, 1908, with the rank of brigadier general. The Hoxies lived at their home on K Street, Washington, overlooking Farragut Square which displayed Vinnie's statue of the famed Admiral. There, her husband had built a private studio for her.

These were busy, crowded days, for even with failing health Vinnie could not be idle. She turned her attention to neighboring youngsters, teaching many of them in her studio to model with clay. She devoted hours to talking with blind boys and girls, and this work brought Vinnie important contacts with similarly interested people in other parts of the world. They included Queen Elizabeth of Romania, wife of King Carol I, who was founding a "city for the blind."

This city Her Majesty describes in a letter to Vinnie from Bucharest, dated May 31, 1907:

My dear Madam,
    You must kindly forgive my not answering sooner your warm, heartfelt, powerful letter, with such a mountain of interest that it did all the uplifting I required in a most painful moment! But I am so overwhelmed with work, that I can scarcely find not only the necessary minutes, but also the thoughts in their proper places! I have even to stop the

typewriter for a time, as the noise fatigues me so.

The only thing that seems to rest me now is a few hours towards evening in the motor, going not very much quicker than a carriage and breathing when the great heat is over. I had the nursing of the King for a whole year, never a quiet night, and many nights on my feet altogether, reading to him half the day, as much as five and six hours, and all my work (as a Queen, not as an author!!) going on as well!

What takes me up completely at the present moment is my city for the blind! Fancy that we have more than 20,000 blind! England has but 10,000! And nothing has been done for them as yet! Happily! Because my idea is just opposite to everything one has done till now. I begin by taking in those who have gone blind, and give them work.

The inventor of the new printing press is at the head of the establishment with his wife and mother-in-law. He is the happy man who can't do without his excellent mother-in-law. She is the widow of a protestant clergyman, and her son is a missionary. I wish I could show you the colony as it is now with near upon a hundred blind, working at eleven different métiers, and the city that is going to be, as soon as the first hundred have done learning and are mostly married.

My city will be a really socialistic one, the first, after all the beautiful plans that have been written, but never executed. I hope it will be the Forest of Arden, dreamt by your dear poet Wright Mabie.

I wish you heard them sing and laugh and make fun together! They arrive in the last stage of despair and are very soon quite happy. I've got an officer, an ingenue, a doctor, an opera singer, merchants, many of them married. And their families are taken in as well. The wives work, the children work and play with the blind children. Blindness is not hereditary, so that we have as many children as we please! —They work eight hours and have music and reading the rest of the time.

When the printing machine will begin to be sold, it will be a large income, as the inventor won't take a penny for himself. I can't tell you how this carried me over the dreadful time of the rising of our peasants! Our harvest threatens to fail! There will be nobody happy in Romania for the next year but the blind! To them there is a haven of rest, after having tested the last and utmost misery!

I send you some photos, also my ex libria, true from nature, which is more to my taste than the complicated designs! It is a part of my home on the Rhine in Monrepos, in the woods that made me sing, where all my graves are, but one, that is here!!

I had three horrors, almost from my earliest childhood: the throne, a house without children and remaining behind alone, when all my beloved went home.—I seem to have known my fate!

If you will send me something for my blind city and get your friends to do the same, you will give me the greatest pleasure. I take in blind of all nations, if they will come. I have got seven languages and seven religions already.

How lovely your work is! I feel the strong pulsation of Life in your letter, of life and creating and feeling successful! Oh! how I wish I could come to America and enjoy all the strong doing there! And yet from my little corner I offer America a new machine! It seems almost unreal!

I hope you will write again!

Yours most truly,
Elizabeth

Particularly, did Vinnie enjoy the visits of the grand-children of those who had been her youthful contemporaries, encouraging many toward a career in the arts. It was still a much-sought-after privilege to be invited to one of "Miss Vinnie's teaparties," for she still dispensed tea every afternoon at four, with hot chocolate for those who preferred it.

Mrs. Coombs of *Mrs. Coombs' Journal*, the Dear Abby of her generation, was once asked to receive with Vinnie at one of her teas. Upon arriving, Mrs. Coombs was somewhat taken aback to find a real flesh-and-blood Indian already installed as the entertainment. The startled guests watched while Vinnie modeled him in clay for her statue of Sequoyah—famous Indian chief who invented the Cherokee alphabet—which was later to represent the state of Oklahoma in the Capitol. Wrote Mrs. Coombs:

> His name is Ishkahula and he looks like a full-blooded Indian, war whoop ready, bow-legged and all. He speaks English quite well and only needed the blanket and war bonnet to be a real Remington red-skin.

Vinnie spent summers with her husband at the old Hoxie homestead at 310 South Lucas Street, Iowa City, which Richard—years before, when they were first married —had named Vinita; ironically, just as Boudy had named his town in her honor. Here in 1914, they spent their last summer together. Fall came and as usual Vinnie, now sixty-seven years old, packed home-grown apples and nuts for less fortunate friends in the city. She went several times to visit Richie at the hospital, then suddenly, one afternoon while walking in her garden, she collapsed. The protective Richard decided to rush her back to Washington where he thought she would receive more skilled medical attention. She traveled with two nurses upon a specially chartered train. The diagnosis was uremic poisoning.

For two months Vinnie lingered in a kind of half-world. Sometimes her mind returned to the days of her youth and she sang the songs that Boudy had taught her. So helpless now, she once asked Richard to carry her into the studio. It was just as she had left it. . . . Governor Kirkwood's plaster bust had gathered a thin covering of dust. Boudy's "dear impudent portrait," hair falling to his shoulders and wearing a wide-brimmed hat, stood next to the Italian urn—a souvenir of her never-to-be-forgotten Carrara journey.

Two days before she died, on November 14th, Vinnie, her face still amazingly young, sang a strange song that Richard had never heard before. He was correct in surmising it to be "something she had learned among the Indians," for Rollin Ridge who, like his cousin Boudy, had loved her long before, had written it:

> By this weird lake we wandered once,
> when life was young and skies were clear,
> the grasses lowly bent their heads,
> the ardent lovers' vows to hear.

Richard buried her in Arlington National Cemetery, Virginia, wearing the bridal gown she had chosen with such care. In her hand he placed the controversial fan.

Over her grave he erected the splendid bronze statue of Sappho, Greek poetess of Lesbos, which Vinnie had modeled. Into the stone below was set a medallion by George Julian Zolnay, the sculptor, showing Vinnie as the simple young girl who had been befriended by Abraham Lincoln. Opposite the statue Richard placed a granite seat, which he said was "intended to typify one of her characteristic traits, a cordial and friendly welcome."

For Vinnie Ream's epitaph he chose:

WORDS THAT WOULD PRAISE THEE ARE IMPOTENT.

Vinnie Ream

* Dulles, Foster Rhea. *The United States Since 1865.* Ann Arbor: University of Michigan Press, 1959.

* Kraus, Michael. *The United States to 1865.* Ann Arbor: University of Michigan Press, 1959.

* Miers, Earl Schenck (ed.). *The American Story: Age of Exploration to the Age of the Atom.* With an introduction by Allan Nevins. Great Neck: Channel Press, 1956.

* Muzzey, David Saville. *A History of Our Country.* Boston: Ginn and Co. 1946. Chapter 17: "Reconstruction."

  * The above four books give background material for the years dealing with the War between the States and the Andrew Johnson impeachment proceedings.

"Art in Arkansas—Sculpture," *Arkansas Historical Quarterly,* Winter issue, 1944. Pp. 324.

Baker, Mrs. Isadore. "The Ream Statue of Farragut," *Carter's Monthly* (Chicago), Vol. XV (May, 1899), 405-410.

——"Vinnie Ream Hoxie: Her Statue of Lincoln and Other Work," *The Midland Monthly,* VIII (November, 1897). This article contains photograph of Vinnie's son Richard Ream Hoxie, wearing a sailor suit.

Barton, William E. *The Women Lincoln Loved.* Indianapolis: The Bobbs-Merrill Company, 1927.

Bayard, Mary Temple. "Vinnie Ream Hoxie," *The Home Monthly,* February, 1898.

Bowers, Claude E. *The Tragic Era: The Revolution After Lincoln.* Cambridge: Houghton Mifflin Co., 1929.

Carr, O. A. (ed.). *Memorial of J. K. Rogers and Christian College,* St. Louis: John Burns Publishing Co., 1885. Pp. 328. Contains various references to Vinnie Ream.

Christ-Janer, Albert. *George Caleb Bingham of Missouri.* New York: Dodd, Mead & Company, Inc., 1940. Contains portrait of Vinnie Ream with her bust of Abraham Lincoln. Pp. 106.

Christian College, Columbia Mo., own various items pertaining to Vinnie Ream, including newspaper clippings from the Columbia Missourian, Columbia Evening Missourian, Kansas City Star, etc.

Dictionary of American Biography, Vol. 9, 317-318. New York: Charles Scribner's Sons, 1932. Biographical data of Vinnie Ream Hoxie.

Fairman, E. E. *Arts and Artists of the Capitol.* 1927.

Family Papers of Joseph Botsford Whitney; Martha Hasseltine Cummings Whitney, Isabel Lydia Whitney, Hasseltine Whitney, and Gordon Langley Hall.

Gerdts, William H. "I Dreamt I Dwelt in Marble Halls: A Century of American Sculpture," *Antiques* Magazine, Vol. LXXXII (No. 2). (August, 1962) 146-149.

Griffin, Maude E. "Vinnie Ream: Portrait of a Sculptor," *Missouri Historical Review*, April, 1962.

Haefner, Marie. "From Plastic Clay," *The Palimpsest* (Iowa City), State Historical Society of Iowa, XI (November, 1930), 473-482. With a portrait of Vinnie Ream by George P. A. Healy.

Hale, Allean Lemmon. *Petticoat Pioneer: The Christian College Story, 1851-1951.* Columbia, Missouri.

Hanaford, Phebe A. *Daughters of America or Women of the Century.* Augusta, Maine: True and Company, New Edition, 1882.

Hoxie, Richard Leveridge. *Vinnie Ream.* Printed privately in Washington, D.C., 1908, and reprinted with additions, 1915, by her husband.

Hoxie, Ruth Norcross. *A Group of Songs, by Vinnie Ream.* Published after Vinnie's death by Ruth Norcross Hoxie, second wife of Richard L. Hoxie. These include "I Love Thee" by Rollin Ridge.

Hoxie Family Papers. For a number of years prior to her death, Ruth Norcross Hoxie presented to the Library of Congress material pertaining to Vinnie Ream Hoxie. This collection is now contained in twelve manuscript boxes and one large portfolio. In addition to the correspondence there are diaries, Vinnie's personal scrapbooks, photographs of Vinnie's sculpture, newspaper clippings, and printed matter.

La Follette's Magazine, Madison, Wisconsin, December, 1914. Contains Vinnie's obituary.

Leech, Margaret. *Reveille in Washington 1860-1865.* New York: Time Incorporated, 1962. (Gives vivid descriptions of Washington, D.C., life during important creative years of Vinnie Ream's life.)

Lomask, Milton. *Andrew Johnson: President on Trial.* New York: Farrar, Straus & Cudahy, Inc., 1960.

Porter, Mrs. Clyde H. "When Lincoln Posed for a 17-Year-Old Missouri Girl to do his Statue," Kansas City Star. February 12, 1939.

Rollins, C. B. "Letters of George Caleb Bingham to James S. Rollins," *Missouri Historical Review,* XXXIII (October, 1938), 73-74.

Taft, Lorado. *The History of American Sculpture.* New York: The Macmillan Co., 1924.

"Vinnie Ream Hoxie," *America's Greatest Men and Women.* Chicago: W. B. Conkey Co., 1894, Vol. 2 (No. 2). Contains a brief biography and an interesting photograph of Vinnie Ream taken in her forties.

"Vinnie Ream Hoxie," *Appleton's Encyclopedia of American Biography,* Vol. 3, 288-289. New York: D. Appleton & Co.

"Vinnie Ream Hoxie," *Who's Who in America.* Chicago: A. N. Marquis & Company, 1914-1915.

Washington Post, November 21, 1914.

The Western Historical Manuscripts Collection, University of

Missouri Library guide reads: "Christian College Papers and Books, 1847-1953. 235 folders, 17 volumes deposited by Christian College . . . There are 10 folders of poems, clippings, etc., concerning Vinnie Ream, noted sculptress and Christian College alumnus . . ."

Georg Morris Brandes

Brandes, Georg Morris. *Reminiscences of My Childhood and Youth.* New York: 1906.

Correspondence Between Georg and Edv. Brandes. Copenhagen: 1939.

Den Unge Brandes (The Young Brandes) by Henger, Copenhagen: 1957.

Elias Cornelius Boudinot

Arkansas Gazette, Little Rock, September 28, 1890.

Chronicles of Oklahoma, Vol. VII. Pp. 502. Contains note of Vinnie Ream Hoxie Memorial Collection.

Gideon, D. C. *Indian Territory.* New York: 1901. Pp. 163. Contains reference to Boudinot and Vinnie Ream. Lewis Pub. Co.

Gould, C. N. *Oklahoma Place Names.* Pp. 68. Vinita (named for Vinnie Ream). University of Oklahoma Press. 1933.

Harmon, S. W. *Hell on the Border.* 1898.

Knight, L. L. *Georgia and Georgians.* 1917.

——*Georgia's Landmarks, Memorials and Legends.* 1913.

Lumpkin, Wilson. *The Removal of the Cherokee Indian from Georgia.* 1907. Printed privately.

Oklahoma: A Guide to the Sooner State. Compiled by Workers of the Writers' Program of the Work Projects Administration in the State of Oklahoma, University of Oklahoma Press, Norman, Okla., 1945. Pp. 221.

Starr, Edward Comfort. *History of Cornwell, Connecticut: A*

Typical New England Town. Cornwall, Connecticut? E. C. Starr? 1926, 156-378.

Thomas, David Y. "Elias Cornelius Boudinot," *Dictionary of American Biography.* Vol. 2. Pp. 479.

Jane Grey Swisshelm

Dictionary of American Biography. New York: Charles Scribner's Sons.

Hanaford, Phebe A. *Daughters of America or Women of the Century.* Augusta, Maine: True and Company, New Edition, 1882. Pp. 683. "Women Journalists."

New York Times, July 23, 1884. Obituary.

Shippee, L. B. "Jane Grey Swisshelm: Agitator," *Mississippi Valley Historical Review,* December, 1920.

Swisshelm, Jane Grey. *Half a Century.* (Autobiography) Privately published, 1865.

The Carnegie Library of Pittsburgh, Pa., has a file on microfilm pertaining to Mrs. Swisshelm's newspaper, *The Pittsburgh Visitor,* which she commenced to publish in January, 1848.